The Paranormal Equation

A New Scientific Perspective on Remote Viewing, Clairvoyance, and Other Inexplicable Phenomena

By James D. Stein, PhD

A division of
The Career Press, Inc.
Pompton Plains, NJ

The Paranormal Equation
Edited and Typeset by Diana Ghazzawi
Cover design by Ian Shimkoviak/theBookDesigners
Printed in the U.S.A.

To order this title, please call toll-free 1-800-CAREER-1 (NJ and Canada: 201-848-0310) to order using VISA or MasterCard, or for further information on books from Career Press.

The Career Press, Inc.
220 West Parkway, Unit 12
Pompton Plains, NJ 07444
www.careerpress.com
www.newpagebooks.com

Library of Congress Cataloging-in-Publication Data

Stein, James D., 1941-

The paranormal equation : a new scientific perspective on remote viewing, clairvoyance, and other inexplicable phenomena / by James D. Stein.

p. cm.

Includes bibliographical references (p.) and index.

ISBN 978-1-60163-228-9 -- ISBN 978-1-60163-589-1 (ebook)

1. Parapsychology. I. Title.

BF1031.S7687 2013

130--dc23

2012023295

Acknowledgments

I'd like to thank three living people—and one who has passed on—in particular for helping to make this book possible. The first of the three who are still with us is my wife Linda, easily the best thing that ever happened to me, and considerably ahead of the second-best, which was moving to California in general and Los Angeles in particular. L.A. isn't what it was (nothing is what it was), but the weather's still great and there's almost nothing you can't do in and around L.A. The second person is my agent, Jodie Rhodes. I've stated in several books that I don't think I'd have a career as a writer had she not been willing to take a chance on me. She seems to know everyone in the publishing field, and in particular she knows the third person I would like to thank: Michael Pye, the publisher of New Page Books. Michael and the others at New Page were willing to take the chance that an orthodox writer could do a pretty good job of presenting a somewhat unorthodox idea. It takes courage to take a risk, especially in today's rather shaky business climate, and I thank Michael and his colleagues for the opportunity to promulgate this idea—other than posting it as one of millions of unread blogs on the Internet.

I never met John Archibald Wheeler, who was a professor of physics at Princeton University until his death in 2008. Wheeler was one of those rare individuals who was willing to look at practically everything with an open mind. In particular, Wheeler regarded physics not just as a set of laws and computational tools for understanding matter and forces, but as a discipline which could reach into other areas of human thought. Wheeler, along with Stephen Hawking, would be chief contenders for the title of best physicist never to win a Nobel Prize. Hawking is more well-known to the general public, but Wheeler is probably more influential. His thoughts and ideas have had a considerable influence in how I wrote this book. I hope that I do nothing to denigrate his memory.

It's time now to start the journey of how science and mathematics have already provided a possible explanation for why there are phenomena in the Universe that lie beyond the power of science to explain.

Contents

Preface

You might be expecting a book with the title *The Paranormal Equation* to start out something like this:

> *There is a small, nondescript building on one of the dusty unnamed roads that criss-cross Area 51. Most of those who actually work in Area 51 have never seen it, and if they opened the door, they would see a bespectacled, middle-aged woman with an out-of-date computer poring over what appear to be purchase orders. If they are curious and look at these, they would find that they actually are purchase orders for the nuts-and-bolts that keep Area 51 going: office supplies, snacks and beverages, etc.*
>
> *But there is a concealed elevator at the back of the room, behind the pictures of current and past American presidents so often found in government offices. That elevator leads to a top-secret subterranean laboratory, where*

> *a team of mathematicians, physicists, and experts in linguistics are poring over a mysterious artifact obtained from the 1947 crash. This artifact appears to be some sort of lightweight plastic, yet it is stronger than titanium. It has resisted all attempts to analyze it, from the chemical tests to which it was subjected when first discovered in 1947, to the magnetic resonance imaging and gas chromatograph tests currently being performed on it—without success.*
>
> *Mysterious symbols flash across its surface, sometimes changing color and arrangement. Videos have been taken of this, and computer analysis of the videos has revealed a pattern to the symbols. It is this pattern on which the mathematicians and linguistic experts have been working. After six decades, they believe they have deciphered it. It is the* Paranormal Equation, *an equation relating the paranormal abilities of our species—telepathy, ESP, and clairvoyance—to the field equations and quantum mechanics which describe the physical Universe.*

Well, that's how this book might begin if it were a science-fiction thriller—but it's not. This is certainly a book about the paranormal and about equations—and also about science, history, and science fiction, with a few of my experiences thrown in. *The Paranormal Equation* was the title for the book that the publisher suggested. Initially, I wasn't too enthusiastic. But after thinking about it, I realized that *The Paranormal Equation* was actually a pretty good descriptive title for the book, because there is a colloquial use of the term *equation* in American society that means "balancing."

Chemists use the term *equation* in somewhat the same sense, in the context of a chemical reaction. A classic chemical reaction occurs when hydrochloric acid, also known as muriatic acid, is mixed with sodium hydroxide, commonly known as lye. The result of this reaction is ordinary table salt and water. The question chemists want to answer is how much hydrochloric acid should be mixed with how much sodium hydroxide in order to obtain a specific quantity of table salt. Ideally, you don't want to have any leftover hydrochloric acid or sodium hydroxide—not just because it would be wasteful, but because both these chemicals are toxic and dangerous. You certainly don't want either of them in the shaker when you're putting salt on scrambled eggs or french fries.

The process of figuring out how much of each ingredient to use in order to obtain a certain quantity of table salt involves a process known as "balancing a chemical equation." It is in this sense that the term *equation* is informally used in contemporary American society. It means a balance of sorts. Can the Republicans balance the equation for a ticket to win the 2012 Presidential election? Can a professional sports team balance the equation for working its way through to the championship? You'll hear the word *equation* appear in these and numerous other contexts, and in that sense I feel that *The Paranormal Equation* is a fair title for the book, because one of the goals of this book is to strike a balance between the believers in paranormal phenomena and the skeptics.

I'd always been interested in the question of why some really top-notch scientists believed in the paranormal and the supernatural; that's part of what this book is about. When you read about them—and you will in this book—you may notice what I did: they often believe in the paranormal or supernatural despite the fact that it goes against their intellect and training to do so. That's rather surprising, especially considering the way the process of science works.

There have been a number of attempts by scientists in good standing to investigate the world of the supernatural and paranormal. It is fair to say that the majority of them have encountered a good deal of resistance from their scientific colleagues on account of those investigations, and this book will present some of the conclusions that they reached. Some of those scientists concluded that there was no validity to the idea of supernatural or paranormal phenomena. Those who reached the conclusion that there was some legitimacy to these ideas often made one of two types of errors. Some of those errors were methodological, such as poorly designed or executed experiments. Another error was that the investigators were the victims of fraud—sometimes obvious, sometimes more subtle. At any rate, some very well-known scientists came to remarkably naïve conclusions when presented with performances claiming to demonstrate some aspect of the supernatural or paranormal, such as communication with the spirit world.

One thing I can say for certain about this book. After reading it, no one will accuse me of being fooled in such a manner—because I have never had a single experience in my life that even remotely smacks of the supernatural or paranormal. I've never seen a ghost. None of my friends or relatives who have died have made any attempts to contact me—at least, not that I know of. My wife sometimes knows what I am thinking—but sometimes not—and I *never* seem to know what she is thinking. One of my friends said that I am the least spiritual person he has ever met. I'm not sure how he intended that, but I took it as a compliment.

However, a few years ago, during the course of writing another book, I suddenly realized that there was a "rational window" for the paranormal and supernatural that I had not seen articulated anywhere. I am convinced that, under hypotheses that are accepted by a significant segment of the scientific community, there are regular, repeatable phenomena that lie beyond the ability of science to validate. Could a Paranormal Equation—in the sense of the thriller I'm not writing—be among them?

Possibly—and that's one of the things you'll read about in this book.

Introduction

We all agree that your theory is crazy. But is it crazy enough?

—Niels Bohr

While I was writing this book, I did some research—some reading and some poking around the Internet. Even the most cursory poking around the Internet will reveal an extraordinary number of Websites that, while paying lip service to the accomplishments of science, claim that they are in possession of deep truths that are beyond the power of science to explain. Many of these deep truths that are beyond the power of science to explain are purported to have life-changing capability and, remarkably, are revealed in books, CDs, DVDs, and seminars promoted by these Websites. To obtain access to these truths, all you generally have to do is shell out some money.

Most of the great scientific truths—and have no doubt, they are indeed great truths, in my opinion the greatest truths that humans have been able to discover—are available for free. Here's what makes them the greatest truths we have been able to discover: as far as we have been able to ascertain, these useful and powerful truths are universal with respect to both space and time. Voltaire once stated, “There are truths which are not for all men, nor for all times.”[1] The great truths of science (and mathematics) are for all men—and for all other species as well—and for all times.

These great truths can be understood with the application of intellectual effort, which is traditionally a whole lot more difficult to summon up than belief. Moreover, these truths do not depend upon belief; in fact, that is one of the contributing factors that makes them great truths. It doesn’t matter whether you believe in Newton’s Third Law or not, what Newton said in his Third Law is true: every action has an equal and opposite reaction. In the sense of Newton’s Third Law, action and reaction are not quantities which are vaguely defined. They are defined precisely, and the statement that every action has an equal and opposite reaction can be phrased as what mathematicians call a one-dimensional vector equation.

There are some great truths of science which are not expressed in mathematical terms, but the greatest of them all are so expressed. Expressing something mathematically has the advantage of allowing quantitative predictions to be made. Not only does this have tremendous practical utility, but it also enables something that is not true to be discarded when experiments show that it gives inaccurate results. That is why the theory of evolution by natural selection, one of the great achievements of science, is not as great a truth as the theory of electromagnetism. There are equations, devised by the brilliant Scottish physicist James Clerk Maxwell, which characterize electromagnetism. These equations have helped enable the incredible panoply of electric and electronic devices which so enrich our lives. No similar equations yet exist for evolution; if there were, there would not be factions arguing that evolution should be taught as a theory, not as established scientific fact. You don't hear anyone arguing that electromagnetism should be taught as a theory rather than established scientific fact.

There was a time in the past, known as the Age of Enlightenment, when it was felt that science could answer all questions. This view is illustrated in the following statement by the French physicist Pierre-Simon de Laplace:

> Given for one instant an intelligence which could comprehend all the forces by which nature is animated and the respective positions of the beings which compose it, if moreover this intelligence were vast enough to submit these data to analysis, it would embrace in the same formula both the movements of the largest bodies in the universe and those of the lightest atom; to it nothing would be uncertain, and the future as the past would be present to its eyes.[2]

We now know that this statement is false, not because of a failure of science, but because of the emergence of chaos theory, a branch of mathematics which has shown that this analysis is technically impossible. Nonetheless, we expect science to be able to answer questions about the forces of Nature; this is the nominal domain of science. These forces of Nature act in a comprehensible fashion, and in doing so establish patterns of behavior—of movement, of electric and magnetic charge, of atomic, chemical, and biological action.

Those who believe in paranormal and supernatural phenomena would disagree to some extent with the previous assertion. They would argue that there are forces that exist that lie beyond the power of science to analyze, and that these forces have a significant impact. The word *force* here is not to be interpreted in a sense external to science, the way a sentence such as "love is the greatest force on Earth" uses the term *force*. Everyone believes that love exists, that it has a power to change things, but I don't think anyone believes that love is a paranormal or supernatural force. The classic example of a presumed paranormal force is the psi force; which will be discussed later and which has been extensively investigated.

This seems like a good time to repeat the claim I made earlier: under a reasonable set of hypotheses, there are regular, repeatable phenomena that lie beyond the ability of science to validate. I do not know whether any of these have life-changing capability; I do not know whether we have already experienced some of these phenomena or if we never will. I will spend some time discussing this, because it bears on a large number of phenomena that are traditionally classified as supernatural or paranormal.

The claim I am making, and will explain in this book, lies completely within the realm of orthodox science and mathematics. What makes it surprising is that it allows a window of opportunity for phenomena currently classified as paranormal or supernatural.

Clarke's Law

Later on in this book you will encounter Arthur C. Clarke, if you haven't encountered him already. Clarke was one of the great science fiction writers, but he also had a great deal of interest in science and the community of scientists. At one stage, he propounded what has come to be known as Clarke's Law: If a distinguished but elderly scientist states that something is possible, he is almost certainly right. When he states that something is impossible, he is very probably wrong.[3]

At least a part of this statement applies to me. Whether or not you consider mathematicians to be scientists, at the very least, I have enough of a background to qualify as a scientist wanna-be. Even if I am allowed to consider myself a scientist, I'm certainly not a distinguished one—but I *am* elderly. Clarke actually states explicitly that mathematicians (he considers them to be scientists) and physicists are elderly if they are more than 30 years old, but chemists and biologists get to postpone senility until they hit 40. I must mention that as of this writing, I'm 70.

The Laugh Test

An idea passes the laugh test if you can state it without laughing. I'm pretty sure that there will be scientists who see the title of this book—*The Paranormal Equation*—and will feel that it has already flunked the laugh test. However, I'm also pretty sure this book has already passed the laugh test even before it was published. Let me explain how.

The last book that I wrote before this one, *Cosmic Numbers*,[4] is a down-the-middle book about science; it discusses the constants such as the speed of light and absolute zero, which delineate our Universe. However, I'm not so well-known an author that all I have to do is say, "I'm writing a book," and publishers line up to try to publish it. I have to write a book proposal and submit it to publishers for reviewing. That's what I did with this one. My agent sent it around to several of the larger publishers. The proposal was read by a number of people, and it attracted a good deal of interest—but no offers. I think that a book dealing with the paranormal, but written by a scientist, made mainstream publishers skittish. However, I did not receive a single comment that the proposal was centered around a ridiculous idea.

I have also discussed this idea with many people who are pursuing careers in math and science. Admittedly, I haven't run it by any of the really heavy hitters in the game, but no one with whom I have discussed the central idea could come up with a strong argument against it. In fact, it actually resonated with several of them, who felt I had articulated something they had intuited. I believe that I've managed to articulate something that many scientists feel, but can't quite put their finger on why they feel it.

This is primarily a book about science. As the cover of the book says, it does contain a new perspective on remote viewing, clairvoyance, and other paranormal phenomena—but it does so within the confines of science.

Science has accomplished amazing things in the brief span of 400 years (I date the birth of science from when Isaac Newton first developed his theories of mechanics and gravitation). We live longer, happier, and better lives because of it. The mission of science is to investigate the natural world. Science has made profound discoveries, and there are doubtless profound discoveries still to be made. There are profound discoveries which will probably never be made, because there are just not enough scientists, the Universe is too large, and as a species we just don't have enough time to make them.

But I believe that there are truths about the natural world that nominally fall within the domain of science that are impossible for science to discover. Of course, I'm not the first one to say this, and I'm not even the first scientist to say this. But I may be the first person to describe a set of circumstances under which there are scientific truths that are impossible for science to discover, and that these truths may be at the heart of some of the phenomena—such as the world of the paranormal—that we consider inexplicable.

Keeping Faith with Science

I'm passionately devoted to science. One book that has greatly influenced me is Carl Sagan's *The Demon-Haunted World: Science as a Candle in the Dark.*[5] Ever since I've been a child, I've been fascinated by science. I've already written several books in which I believe this love of science and mathematics comes through. I would never, ever write a book that I thought would add to the number of demons haunting the world.

Like it or not—and there are many scientists who don't—there are many people who are interested in the paranormal and the supernatural. While writing this book, it occurred to me that I can get those people who are interested in the paranormal and the supernatural to learn something about science by discussing what science really has to say about what they believe—especially when it has something to say that may help to support some of their ideas.

At this moment, any scientist reading this book may have a hard time believing that science has anything to say that might support belief in either the supernatural or the paranormal. I hope I can convince him or her otherwise. A good starting point would be for scientists to ask themselves why some of the greatest scientists in history have not only believed in these matters, but have been willing to investigate it from a scientific standpoint.

There are those scientists who are so completely convinced that they have the right slant on a particular subject that they are willing to stand alone against the consensus viewpoint. Many of the great discoveries of science have been made this way. Science is a highly conservative activity, and it goes to a lot of trouble to verify that something deserves the appellation "scientific knowledge." As a result, bucking the prevailing viewpoint requires both conviction and courage. I have the conviction but not the courage, so it was gratifying to find that the distinguished physicist John Archibald Wheeler spent some time looking at topics related to the idea that I am going to present in this book. In view of what I have read about Wheeler, I think he would look at the main idea of this book with an open mind.

And so, I hope, will all readers, skeptics and non-skeptics alike.

Belief and Understanding

This is a book about that portion of the Universe that technically lies within the domain of what science traditionally analyzes, but lies beyond the power of science to understand. Whether or not there even is such a portion of the Universe is a matter for debate, although my guess is that the majority of non-scientists, perhaps even the great majority, believe this to be true. At any rate, in this book, the reader will meet some of those who feel that what you see is what you get, as far as the Universe is concerned. The reader will also meet some of those who feel that there is indeed a portion of the Universe that lies beyond the power of science to understand. However, the people the reader will encounter in this book are not oriental mystics or New Age thinkers; they're scientists. Most of this book is not about belief, or feeling. It's about hard data, reason, and understanding.

One of the chief differences between belief and understanding is what happens when these two modes of thinking collide with reality. Understanding invariably gets modified when a "reality check" occurs. There is nothing so uncomfortable for a scientist as when a beautiful theory collides with an ugly fact, for it is the beautiful theory that must be modified to accommodate the ugly fact. As the noted scientist Richard Feynman said during the investigation of the *Challenger* disaster, "For a successful technology, reality must take precedence over public relations, for nature cannot be fooled."[6]

That's not necessarily the case when reality collides with belief systems. In fact, reality that seems at odds with a belief system sometimes strengthens belief. The measure by which a believer is judged is sometimes not the accuracy of the belief, but the strength with which the believer can hold on to that belief, even when reality appears to conflict with that belief. This is sometimes an extremely good thing, as great deeds have been accomplished because people have continued to believe under great duress. Great deeds have been accomplished under these conditions—but never great science.

What Do We Mean by *Paranormal* and *Supernatural*?

In the article *Is Parapsychology a Science?*,[7] Paul Kurtz states something that we all know: the very meaning of the terms *paranormal* and *supernatural* are unclear. There are presumed phenomena such as ESP, precognition, and psychokinesis, which certainly qualify for these terms. However, there's a bunch of other stuff that is clumped under these headings that basically is just weird. This includes UFOs, alien abductions, spontaneous combustion, ghosts, and a host of other subjects.

I'm not going to spend much time on the weird stuff. Not because that stuff is weird, but because the science I know simply doesn't spend much time on something if you can't make repeated observations. (It's even better if you can do experiments.) Repeated observations enable us to establish scientific laws—some of which are explanatory, and some of which are quantitative. Though we can control what happens when we do experiments in chemistry and can't control what happens when we make observations in astronomy, in both cases we have regular, repeatable phenomena to work with—so science can get somewhere. On the other hand, science hasn't put in a whole lot of time on alien abductions, because 1) there's a great deal of skepticism about whether any alien abductions have ever taken place, and 2) even if they have, where do you go from there? It's hard for science to work solely on descriptions of personal experiences.

Science can get close to the truth, but science can never prove anything completely. Maybe that's why mathematics is sometimes not felt to be a science, because in mathematics you can prove things completely. You'll never find a right triangle in which the square of the hypotenuse is unequal to the sum of the squares of the other two sides. That great truth was first proved by Pythagoras more than 2,000 years ago, and it is unequivocal.

As a result, scientists are generally fairly careful about making a statement such as "there is no such thing as telepathy." Science cannot demonstrate that there is no such thing as telepathy. All scientists know that, and most scientists will hedge their bets when uttering such a statement. They will say something like, "Based on what we currently understand about science, it is extremely unlikely that there is such a phenomenon as telepathy." This is not to be construed as "wimping out," it's just that scientists realize that scientific truth is one level below mathematical truth. It's the best we can do—at the moment—but it's subject to revision.

Albert Einstein put it in exactly these terms in a letter he wrote to Jan Ehrenwald, who studied and wrote about psi phenomena for three decades in the first half of the 20th century. Einstein said, "It seems to me, at any rate, that we have no right, from a physical standpoint, to deny *a priori* the possibility of telepathy. For that sort of denial the foundations of our science are too unsure and too incomplete."[8]

Einstein had probably never heard of Clarke's Law, but his statement is certainly a classic example of it. Einstein was the quintessence of the distinguished but elderly scientist; you can't get more distinguished than Einstein, and he made that statement in his later years. The above statement, that we cannot deny the possibility of telepathy, qualifies as a statement that telepathy is possible. Until we rule it out, it is possible.

But lots of things are possible—even things that you will never experience. Here's a simple example of something that is possible and that you have never seen, and never will: you have never seen ice cubes form spontaneously in a glass of warm water (unless some outside form of refrigeration is applied). Although it is theoretically possible, the Universe would have to last a gazillion times longer than it actually has in order for an event like this to pass from the realm of "not completely impossible" to "just very barely possible." I've used the word "gazillion" even though it is not a specific number in order to convey the idea of just how unlikely this event is.

I hope that by the end of this book I will have convinced you that there are hypotheses that are accepted by a reasonable number of mainstream scientists which lead to the conclusion that there are regular, repeatable phenomena that science will never be able to verify and may not even be able to discover. I don't know if that fits your definition of paranormal or supernatural phenomena, but it does fit mine, as well as the dictionary's.

Quantum Smoke and Mirrors

As I mentioned, since I got the idea for this book, I have visited a number of Websites discussing the supernatural and the paranormal. With almost no exceptions, whenever you see a claim such as "quantum physics supports the existence of paranormal or supernatural phenomena," the Website has absolutely no idea what it is talking about.

Quantum mechanics, which I will discuss in this book, is a profound and beautiful theory which presents a very different view of reality than the one to which we are generally accustomed. It talks about concepts which have occasionally been viewed as consistent with ideas long espoused by oriental philosophies and religions, or with ideas currently being promulgated by mystics and New Age thinkers (whatever that means). I believe that an intelligent discussion of quantum mechanics is an integral component of this book, but you will never find an intelligent discussion of quantum mechanics on any of those Websites.

What are my credentials for discussing quantum mechanics? I got a B+ in an upper-division course in it—while at college I majored in math and minored in physics. Since then, I have read extensively about it. I understand some of it, nowhere near as much as a competent physicist. However, I do understand enough to know that the vast majority of Websites that use the word *quantum* while discussing the paranormal or the supernatural are trying to get the visitor to that Website to buy into what they are selling. And make no mistake, they are generally selling something: books, CDs, training systems—you name it.

Oh, yes, full disclosure: I'm selling something, too, but I believe it has the support of mathematics and logic. I'll lay it all out without trying to pull the wool over your eyes by saying something like "recent discoveries in quantum physics support this."

Stranger Than We Can Imagine

I'm not expecting everyone who reads this book to buy into the idea I am going to present, but I think I can make a damned good case for it. The history of science is that wrong ideas often lead to correct ideas, but the absence of ideas never leads anywhere. Presenting this idea is an unusual form of a win-win situation. If I'm wrong, I would be delighted to see it demonstrated, as maybe it would lead the way to some right ideas. Having a stupendously bad idea is occasionally even more productive than having a pretty good idea. If I'm stupendously wrong, there will be a lot to be learned in demonstrating that I'm wrong. In fact, if I'm really wrong, it will strengthen the case for the orthodox scientific view of the Universe—and I think that's a tremendous service to increasing knowledge and decreasing ignorance. That's a big win for science. And if I'm right, we live in a Universe that is, as the distinguished astronomer Sir Arthur Eddington said, not only stranger than we imagine, but is stranger than we can imagine.[9] That's a big win for awe and wonder, and for knowing that there are indeed limits for what we can expect science to disclose.

Under the Hood

If all you want to do is to learn how to drive a car, all you need to do is learn how and when to push the appropriate pedals, and how and when to turn the steering wheel. However, if you really want to understand how a car works, you have to look under the hood.

I'm presenting an idea that has a lot to do with mathematics, and although I don't expect everyone who reads the book to go "under the hood," I want those readers who intend to examine the idea deeply to be able to do so. That means that I need to devote some time to developing the idea in a technical fashion. There are a few technical discussions that I feel are an important part of the book—but not everyone has to go "under the hood." However, I think most of it is easily understood without too much in the way of technical background.

But if a technical discussion bores or bothers you, feel free to skip it. You won't lose much by doing so. For instance, most of us use a lot of science and technology without bothering to know how it works. I have no idea, other than a vague one, of how my car works; it's good enough that the engine starts when I turn the key in the ignition and that there are people around who can repair it when something goes wrong. However, just as there are those people who want to know how a car works, there are people who want to know the rationale behind what math and science have to say, and so I've included some of the details. If math bothers you, don't worry; I mostly talk about it rather than do it. A lot of people who hate math enjoyed the show *Numb3rs.*

The core idea of this book is that science and mathematics have already provided the tools for a plausible explanation of why supernatural phenomena should exist. Because many of those who read this book will not have the background to understand or appreciate the idea, it's up to me to supply that background. I think I can do a pretty good job of that; a math teacher gets a lot of experience explaining ideas in a way that students who are being exposed to the ideas for the first time can understand them.

1 The Known, the Unknown, and the Unknowable

I was born into a family which was basically non-religious. We lived in suburban New York, and all our neighbors and my playmates were Catholic, but we weren't. We celebrated Christmas by giving gifts and eating a turkey dinner, and because Santa Claus was coming to give me (and the other kids) presents, I didn't see much reason to go more deeply into the matter. I didn't go to church or Sunday school, and religion and the topics related to religion never came up as a subject for discussion, either with my parents or with my playmates. As a result, the topic of "life after death" never even occurred to me—until the daily newspaper started serializing the story of Bridey Murphy.

Bridey Murphy represented my first foray into the world of the paranormal and the supernatural, but like all my other such forays, it didn't happen directly to me. The Bridey Murphy story occurred in the 1950s, and unless you are a devotee of such material, you're probably not familiar with it. A Colorado housewife named Virginia Tighe was put under hypnosis and subjected to a procedure known as past-life regression, where she was encouraged to recall events that happened to her before she was born. While under hypnosis, she started describing her experiences as Bridey Murphy, an Irish woman born centuries earlier. I think the current term for this is *channeling*, although it was not used at the time. The story of Bridey Murphy was front-page stuff in the papers. It was serialized over weeks, it was fascinating, and I read it avidly. However, with time, doubts began to grow about the veracity of Tighe's experience. Though probably not formally a hoax in the sense that Bridey Murphy was deliberately constructed with the intent to deceive, most scientists today are convinced that Bridey Murphy was merely an offshoot of long-forgotten childhood memories of descriptions given by a woman named Bridie Murphey Corkell, who turned out to be a long-forgotten neighbor from Tighe's childhood. I don't recall whether experts were consulted to give their opinion as sidebars to the serialized version that I read, but there was no question that it made extremely interesting reading. Others must have found it so as well, because the serialized version of the story lasted several weeks. It certainly piqued my curiosity regarding a phenomenon I hadn't even considered until I read the story. However, the eventual debunking of the story helped to shape my view of supernatural and paranormal phenomena. This viewpoint was reinforced by my emerging interest in science and mathematics. I'm generally only satisfied by rigorous scientific proof or verifiable documentation. Until I see that, I'm not going to believe in reincarnation—or ghosts, or UFOs, or out-of-body experiences.

I'm a very left-brained individual. I also think I'm fairly typical in that most of my friends tend to be like me; after all, nerds hang out with other nerds, jocks with jocks, and artists with artists. Often we're attracted to people with whom we share common interests, and because we share common interests, we often tend to think alike on a wide variety of subjects. Many of my friends are mathematicians, doctors, scientists, and engineers; we're generally a pretty hard-headed, left-brained, and rational a collection of human beings. Yet several of these left-brained people have beliefs in supernatural or paranormal phenomena: things, events, or processes that go considerably beyond what are currently the bounds of science. The brightest mathematician I know believes in reincarnation. One of my good friends, a Harvard-educated doctor with impeccable research credentials, has told me that he has walked into a room and known what's in the room before ever having been there. I've never had an experience even remotely like that; I'm often sufficiently oblivious that I can walk into a room and not know what's in it even while I'm there. I have no doubt that my friend genuinely believes he has had this experience, especially because he has told me it has occurred to him several times.

Although my friend is firmly convinced he has had these experiences, I believe there's a straightforward explanation. Either he'd seen a picture of the room or had heard someone describe it, and he had simply forgotten the incident. My guess is that if one were to carefully scrutinize all the incidents similar to this, one would find that the vast majority had simple explanations. To a certain extent, I think these incidents would resemble the findings that have been compiled with respect to UFO sightings. Most UFO sightings can be explained in a fairly straightforward fashion—but there are a few for which no straightforward explanation is satisfactory. I suspect we'd find the same for instances of *déjà vu*, such as my friend has experienced. However, it's important to realize that just because we haven't found the straightforward explanation does not mean that no straightforward explanation exists.

My two friends are just the latest in a long line of scientists who have a belief in the supernatural and the paranormal. A study of respected scientists brings up a surprising number who believe in supernatural or paranormal phenomena. There have been a number of highly reputable scientists who not only have a belief in the supernatural or paranormal, but have pursued this belief in conjunction with their scientific career. So let's meet the current poster child for this group.

Brian Josephson

Brian Josephson shared the Nobel Prize in 1973 for the discovery of the Josephson Effect, which involves the behavior of a type of junction between two superconductors, later to be known as a Josephson junction. These junctions have important practical applications; they enable ultra-high-speed computation and are used in encephalographic studies of the brain.

Josephson made his key discovery while quite young, which might have been predicted because he was an exceptionally distinguished undergraduate. One of his professors recalled that it was necessary to prepare lectures with extreme precision in courses in which Josephson was a student, for if an error took place, Josephson would wait until the end of class and then very politely point out the mistake to the professor.

Other scientists have won Nobel Prizes; other scientists have shown exceptional talent at an early age. However, Josephson has something else in common with many scientists, past and present: he shares an interest and belief in paranormal and supernatural phenomena. He has published papers on relationships between quantum mechanics and the paranormal. When someone as demonstrably brilliant as Josephson, and the other scientists who share his belief in paranormal phenomena, believe a subject is worthy of serious investigation, I don't think you can simply dismiss it.

Fraud

Although I'm live-and-let-live when it comes to beliefs, I'm strongly opposed to fraud. And there's a lot of fraud going around.

Although the textbook picture of science is of earnest and passionate seekers of truth, the simple fact is that there's a certain amount of scientific fraud, and for generally the same reason that fraud occurs in other areas—personal gain. Grants are awarded and prestige is gained as the result of research, and there is a temptation (fortunately which is resisted by most scientists) to produce dramatic results even at the cost of accuracy.

However, scientific fraud is almost invariably discovered, simply because science has a built-in mechanism for exposing fraud. The experiments leading up to a dramatic discovery can generally be performed by others. Indeed, the really dramatic discoveries are almost always accompanied by such checking. Although this procedure is generally used to detect unintentional errors, it can also be used to expose fraud.

But the amount of fraud in science is a drop in the bucket compared with the amount of fraud, nonsense, and charlatanry associated with the study of the supernatural. Not only that, but there is one real problem that those who believe in the supernatural or the paranormal have yet to surmount: they have yet to come up with any evidence of any supposed supernatural or paranormal phenomenon—ghosts, UFOs, telepathy, whatever—that would stand up in a court of law, much less withstand serious scientific scrutiny. In later chapters I will look at some of the distinguished scientists of the past and present who have either stated a belief in paranormal or supernatural phenomena, or have actually investigated them. All scientists are every bit as skeptical as I am when it comes to scientific matters. The standard of proof required for something to be part of accepted scientific knowledge is extraordinarily high. Yet many scientists believe in supernatural or paranormal phenomena, knowing that the actual evidence for such phenomena is probably not even enough to budge the evidence needle off zero. As we'll see, some of those scientists were clearly the victims of fraud—but not all of them.

Although I have never met Brian Josephson, I am certain that he knows all this, as do all the other distinguished scientists who believe in such matters. To quote from the lyrics of a song by Buffalo Springfield, "Something's happening here, what it is ain't exactly clear."[1] Just why do all these scientists (to say nothing of other highly intelligent individuals) believe in phenomena for which there is no solid evidence?

There are several standard reasons for belief. The most obvious is personal experience; if you think you have seen a ghost, you undoubtedly believe in ghosts. Another is that you feel there is sufficient anecdotal evidence from others, even though you may not personally have experienced same. Many people who believe in UFOs have not personally seen a UFO, but so many other people have, or are under the impression that they have, that it convinces those without direct personal experience. A third is a sense that this is the way the world must or should be: I believe the Chicago Cubs will win a World Series, despite all evidence to the contrary.

Math and Myth

There is virtually no fraud in the development of mathematics the way there is in science. This is due to two factors. The first is that the development of mathematics is generally 99 percent intellectual effort, and the results of that effort can be readily checked. The second is that there just aren't the huge sums of money awaiting mathematical breakthroughs the way there are scientific breakthroughs. There are a few, though. The Clay Institute has offered prizes of a million dollars each for the solution of some extremely important mathematical problems, but this pales in comparison to the money that could be made from the development of the best way to create schedules. This, however, pales in comparison with the amount of money that could be made from developing a cure for the common cold.

Fraud in mathematics usually comes not from doing it, but either from not doing it or convincing other people that math says something other than what it actually does. There are truth-in-advertising laws now, but generally when I hear someone say "do the math," the next thing I hear is that the results of the math support whatever product or service is being pitched. The math might well be correct, but I'm a little suspicious.

Until maybe a decade ago, math had an extremely low public profile—and what people knew or felt they knew about mathematics and mathematicians was generally wrong. Studies were done which showed that people felt they knew a lot more about mathematics than they actually did, and they also felt that their abilities in math were generally much higher than they actually were. A significant segment of the population felt that Albert Einstein was a mathematician—he was actually a physicist. In fact, Einstein once said, "Do not worry about your difficulties in mathematics. I can assure you mine are still greater."[2]

Times change. Since then, there have been works of entertainment which present mathematics—and mathematicians—in a favorable light. Movies such as *Good Will Hunting* and *A Beautiful Mind*, and television shows such as *Numb3rs*, while presenting a somewhat exaggerated view of what mathematics and mathematicians can do, nonetheless have acquainted a large number of people with the scope of mathematics. Many people who previously had thought that mathematics basically consists of balancing the checkbook now realize that mathematics plays a significant role in helping us to create new technology and to better understand the world.

However, there's a downside to the increased popularity of math. What math is capable of doing is often greatly exaggerated, and there are serious misunderstandings concerning this. I'll discuss this further in later chapters. The flip side of this is that stuff that math is capable of doing—and should be doing—is frequently ignored. I'll discuss that as well, because one of the things that math is capable of doing is using statistics to analyze claims. A lot of this has been done in regard to some of the material that is the subject of this book, and I think it's important to be aware of this material.

How I Happened to Write This Book

One of the reasons that I feel I can bring some balance to the Paranormal Equation is that I respect people who have different beliefs from mine. Someone once said that it is better to light a single candle than to curse the darkness, but I believe that was written for a different era than the one in which we now live. Currently, it is a lot more popular—and profitable—to loudly curse the darkness. Extreme right-wingers write books on how liberals are Satan incarnate, while extreme left-wingers write books on how right-wingers will destroy both America and the planet. The same thing happens with regard to the Paranormal Equation. Although I have a tremendous respect for Carl Sagan and all the others who believe that the supernatural and the paranormal are simply unproven and unsubstantiated anecdotes, I also don't think that you can simply say that Brian Josephson and the others who share his views are off the rails.

However, for most of my life, the Paranormal Equation hadn't even entered my mind. I had reached the conclusion that the supernatural and paranormal were unproven and unsubstantiated anecdotes—I'll describe some of my experiences later in the book—but it wasn't really a big deal for me. I had also had some discussions with some of my friends who had a different viewpoint; because I respected them I respected their viewpoint, but it wasn't mine.

And then, several years ago, I was in the process of writing another book,[3] when I suddenly had the idea on which this book is based.

That book was primarily about the application of mathematics to prove that there are things we are incapable of accomplishing. I've already discussed in the Introduction one thing we are not capable of accomplishing, and that is Laplace's vision of the ultimate "clockwork Universe." Even if we know where everything is and where it's going, we cannot predict where it will be. As an example, we think of the orbits of planets as being completely determined—but we cannot predict on which side of the Sun Pluto will be thousands of years from now (yes, I know Pluto is not presently considered to be a planet, but it was for most of my life).

Math is capable of describing amazing things about the Universe in which we live. It tells us a lot about the world in which we live. Math deals with abstractions, some of which do not as yet have practical uses, but which may someday be employed for purposes which may be of immense benefit to humanity. The utility of apparently abstract mathematical ideas has been demonstrated frequently in the past. In the latter portion of the 19th century, a number of mathematicians were spending a lot of time on a subject known as differential geometry. At the time, differential geometry was simply a way to study surfaces, and had little or no practical uses. Enter Albert Einstein, who recognized that differential geometry had come up with precisely the right way to present his General Theory of Relativity.

Math is the major intellectual tool that science has at its disposal to describe and predict. That's the primary use to which science puts math. However, math also has the capacity to delimit science, to say (as in the case of the orbit of Pluto) what science is not capable of doing.

It's obvious that there are certain things that science is not capable of analyzing, because science deals with measurable quantities, and some things are just not measurable. You can digitize the Gettysburg Address, you can transmit it electronically at close to the speed of light from practically anywhere to practically anywhere else, but science cannot explain why it provokes such strong feelings by simply counting the words and letters. For example, you can get the same information content from the following two sentences:

1. Fourscore and seven years ago, our fathers brought forth upon this continent a new nation, conceived in liberty and dedicated to the proposition that all men are created equal.
2. This country was founded 87 years ago on the principle of equality.

The second sentence is better—at least from the standpoint of efficiency. It uses fewer words to transmit the same information. However, it's possible that nobody would have even bothered to listen to the Gettysburg Address had Lincoln started out by saying, "This country was founded 87 years ago on the principle of equality." I doubt that science will ever be able to explain why the first sentence is so moving and the second one merely a dull recitation of fact; it sure can't do so now.

So merely saying that there are things that happen in the Universe that science is incapable of analyzing is a non-starter in the world of interesting ideas. But science is capable of analyzing Nature. In fact, that's basically what science does, and it does it incredibly well. Science and technology are primarily responsible for making the world an enjoyable place for us to live in: most of those who will read this book live in reasonable accommodations, eat well (perhaps too well), enjoy reasonable health, and have a lifestyle that would be envied by the great kings and emperors who lived any time before the 20th century, as that's the time that technology really took off.

There are those who hold to the view that science explains all about Nature, or at least has the capacity to do so. There are also those who believe that there are things in Nature that happen but which defy objective scientific explanation. Such things are generally referred to as supernatural.

The term *supernatural* casts a wide net. Almost everyone would classify anything in the realm of "life after death," such as communications with individuals who have died, as supernatural. After all, dead is dead—or is it?

Also generally thought of as being in the supernatural ballpark are ghosts, ESP, alien abductions, and a host of other subjects. For the most part, this book is not about life after death or ghosts—although they do get more than a passing mention. It's about things that happen—or could happen—in Nature that go beyond the power of science to explain.

Nature refers to the physical or material world. Some of the topics conventionally thought of as supernatural are definitely in the Nature ballpark: for instance, ESP (an acronym for extrasensory perception), which is the ability to perceive things without the direct use of one's five senses. During the period from the 1930s through the 1970s, Professor Joseph Banks Rhine of Duke University performed an extensive series of experiments in an attempt to determine whether certain individuals had the ability to perceive which symbols are on a deck of cards. We will discuss these experiments and their results later, but whatever is happening (or not happening) in these experiments is a part of Nature. There are obviously two questions that need to be considered. First, is ESP a real phenomenon? Second, if ESP is a real phenomenon, is it one that could be explained by science?

One theme that will occur throughout this book is that just because science does not explain it now does not mean that science will never be able to explain it. And this is one of the great problems that one faces in confronting whether things can or cannot be supernatural. Can we know that we are confronting something that science will never be able to explain?

One of my friends told me that the Universe contained three types of facts: the known, the unknown, and the unknowable. It sounds a little like channeling Donald Rumsfeld, the former Secretary of Defense, who discussed the unknown unknowns one encounters in the course of preparing military action.[4] I couldn't resist the reference to the Rumsfeld remark, but the categorization into known, unknown, and unknowable is pivotal to this book.

The supernatural falls into the category of the unknowable. If we knew it, it wouldn't be supernatural, would it? And if it were just unknown, might we not get around to it sooner or later? These are important questions, and I'll go into them in more detail in a later chapter.

Although at the time I was writing the book about how math explains the world the phrase *Paranormal Equation* hadn't even occurred to me, I suddenly realized that the idea that had occurred to me might provide a middle-ground resolution to the ongoing battle between the hard-headed realists and the people who believe in the paranormal. Suppose that I were able to convince people that mathematics has already produced the tools which, in conjunction with science, explain that under a reasonable set of hypotheses which would be accepted by many scientists, supernatural phenomena must exist. This would be a position that almost certainly would be acceptable to both sides.

I've also mentioned that I've run my idea by some scientist types, and scientists constitute one of the two types of individuals who are the most likely audience for this book. If a hard-headed scientist reads this book, there is a good chance that he or she is itching to point out some major error that I have made which completely invalidates my line of reasoning. Frankly, that's the way the science game is played: you put an idea out there and let everybody take their best shot. I know that if someone else had written this book, that's the way I would read it—if I read it at all! The second type of individual is probably someone who has a belief in the supernatural, and is interested in why a scientist should suddenly have a change of heart.

This book presents an approach to the existence of supernatural phenomena that I haven't seen explicitly articulated anywhere, although it's certainly possible it has occurred to someone else. However, it is my contention that many of the scientists who believe in supernatural phenomena have reached this conclusion for reasons similar to ones that I will outline in this book. The "reasonable hypotheses" I refer to above are accepted by many scientists. I believe that many of the scientists who believe in supernatural phenomena are subconsciously aware of the mathematics and the hypotheses necessary to support their belief; they simply haven't consciously "done the math," which is relatively straightforward, to actually crank out this result. In this book, we'll do the math that I believe forms the foundation for the reason that there are scientists who believe in the supernatural. Don't worry; here "doing the math" isn't going to require you to solve quadratic equations or anything of that ilk. It's necessary to do it for the sake of completeness—and also to satisfy those scientist types who are itching to prove me wrong. But, as I said in the Introduction, if you don't want to tough out the math, you can skip those sections and cut to the chase.

The Realm of the Weird

You might think that since this idea occurred to me, I have changed my position on reincarnation, ghosts, UFOs, or out-of-body experiences. I haven't, for reasons that will become clear later. You might recall that in the Introduction I talked about alien abductions as being in the realm of the weird. This book isn't about the realm of the weird; it's about the stuff that science studies: matter, force, energy, and information. That may not seem like the stuff from which one can manufacture the supernatural or the paranormal, but I believe that I can convince you that it can.

Although I'm not a well-known writer, I have written a number of books about math and science. All of them are straightforward narratives of the accomplishments of mathematics and science, and the individuals who played key roles in these achievements. Although I have speculated somewhat on future developments, these speculations are within the framework of science.

As a mathematician with a passionate love for science, I want to make it clear from the outset that this is primarily a book about science. Nonetheless, I have reached the conclusion that there are phenomena that occur in the Universe that fit the definition of supernatural: they occur in conjunction with natural laws that science will never be able to explain. They are genuinely and demonstrably unknowable. I'm going to go out on a limb here and say that if and when someone produces a documented report of a ghost, and ghosts turn out to be genuine phenomena, that science will be able to analyze and understand them, and ghosts will then prove not to be supernatural.

In addition, I believe there are phenomena that qualify as supernatural that do not require life for their existence. Though life isn't in the realm of the weird, a lot of stuff that possibly gets associated with life definitely belongs to the realm of the weird. Take ghosts, for example. Ghosts are dead (or the spirits of the dead, whatever that means), and death requires life. Science is in its infancy in general—it's really only been around as a formal discipline for less than four centuries, but it's embryonic when it comes to describing living things (or dead things), which are vastly more complex than the inanimate things that sciences such as physics, chemistry, and astronomy are more comfortable in describing.

So if you've picked up this book in the hopes of finding evidence for ghosts or reincarnation, I'm sorry to disappoint you. But I think you'll be rewarded in a different way. If you're a believer in the supernatural, you'll find that I am, too—at least, under certain hypotheses. However, my supernatural may not be the same as yours; in fact, it's very probably not the same as yours. I don't think you'll ever get me to believe in ghosts unless you show me a repeatable set of circumstances in which documented ghosts appear. The same goes for alien abductions and life after death. However, I do believe that there are phenomena that occur in the Universe that we think science should be able to explain, but which are demonstrably beyond the power of science to explain. Moreover, some of the things that are conventionally thought of as supernatural or paranormal could fall into this category. Coming from a really hard-headed "you've got to show me" type such as myself, that amounts to a serious conversion.

The Realm of the Universe

Because this is a book about science, you're going to learn some science—more if this isn't an area that's familiar to you, less if you already know a lot, but you'll almost certainly learn something. As Carl Sagan put it in his wonderful book *The Demon-Haunted World*, science is a candle in the dark. It is the only way that we can learn about the way the Universe is, through theorizing and experimentation to determine whether those theories are correct. If, after you have gained a basic understanding of science, you still wish to believe in demons (whatever they are), feel free to do so, but I would hope that the demons in which you believe are consistent with what science has disclosed about the Universe. I cannot imagine that I would ever espouse a position inconsistent with the discoveries of science, as I will go to my grave believing that in many ways these discoveries are the finest intellectual achievement of our species. As I said in the Introduction, I believe that if I can get people to learn more about science and appreciate it for the magnificent intellectual and practical edifice that it is, I'll have accomplished something genuinely worthwhile. Yes, even if I have to talk about the paranormal to do it!

Let's look at gravity. I'll be spending a fair amount of time in this book looking at gravity. You may wonder why, but I have a good reason for doing so. According to the latest version of physics, there are four forces: gravity, electromagnetism, and the strong and weak nuclear forces. Our theories about gravity are pretty good; Newton came up with the first one, and it works very well in all sorts of normal situations. It doesn't work so well at velocities that are exceptionally fast, such as when an object nears the speed of light, or with objects that are incredibly dense, such as neutron stars or black holes. Einstein's Theory of Relativity has improved upon Newton's. Both theories tell us that if you drop something here on planet Earth, it's going to fall down and it's not going to rise up. If someone tells you they have sufficient psychokinetic powers that if you drop a nail they can make it rise to the ceiling, and they drop a nail and it does indeed rise to the ceiling, even if you believe that the mind has unbelievable and untapped powers, you would probably wonder whether there was a strong electromagnet concealed in the ceiling that was activated by a hidden switch. That's because you already have enough knowledge of science to cause you to become skeptical. As a result, you're less likely to be fooled. True, science engenders skepticism, but science can also confirm belief. Science doesn't care what you believe or what you don't; its goal is to find out the way things are.

Your Least-Favorite Subject

When I'm introduced to someone, I usually describe myself as a teacher, because that's how I think of myself. Years ago, if the person to whom I was introduced was an attractive young lady, and if she cared enough to pursue the introduction further and asked what I taught, I would smile a rueful smile and say, "Your least-favorite subject." Almost always, she would say, "Oh, you teach math."

In addition to learning some science, you're also going to learn about mathematics. Notice that I said you're going to learn *about* mathematics, rather than saying you're going to learn mathematics. This is not a math book. I can hear the barely audible sighs of relief. In the rare instances where I actually go to the trouble of doing a little mathematics—and I assure you these are indeed rare instances—feel free to skip the explanations. They're not essential for you to understand the idea that I'm presenting, but I do need to include a little math for the sake of completeness.

Mathematics and logical reasoning are the only forms of guaranteed knowledge that we have. Some of our scientific theories are excellent, having been confirmed through experiments to an extraordinary precision. But there is still a margin for error: if a scientific theory has been confirmed to an accuracy of .00001, it may fail with one more decimal point of precision. This has happened before, and will unquestionably happen again. But mathematics and logical reasoning, correctly applied, are never wrong.

You may wonder if I'm going to describe a situation which cannot characterize our Universe. The answer to that is a resounding *no.* As I said, I need to make some hypotheses, but the hypotheses that I make could definitely characterize our Universe, and many scientists believe that they do. (I'll identify some of these scientists later.) True, the mathematics in this book is definitely not covered in school (which is why I'll talk about it but spare you most of the clinical details), but I believe the conclusions have distinct consequences for the Universe in which we live. Moreover, those conclusions accord well with those who believe that there is something ineffable about the Universe. So, if you're already a believer in the supernatural or the paranormal, they're the kind of conclusions you'll endorse.

2 Secondhand Encounters With the Paranormal

Fraud is the deliberate falsifying of information in order to gain something by doing so. However, there are a lot of people who give out false or misleading information without doing so fraudulently, because they sincerely believe they are right. Scientists are every bit as capable of being wrong as anyone else; but the difference is that science has a mechanism which helps to steer it in the direction of truth. That mechanism is not always employed, and when it is used it is sometimes used incorrectly, but it is there and is fundamental to the functioning of science.

Up until a few years ago, if I had seen a book (or TV show or magazine article) with the title *The Paranormal Equation,* I would have thought it was the work of a con artist. I have a reverence for equations, and knowing that there is no Paranormal Equation in the strict mathematical sense, I would have smelled a rat. Math is sometimes used to bedazzle people; its symbols and sentences look mysterious and incomprehensible to those who don't understand them. I have seen examples in which math is used to take advantage of people who are ignorant of mathematics. Such an event happened to a friend of mine about eight years ago.

Invitation to a Seminar

I have known Linda for 30 years. She is a good friend and an extremely talented jewelry designer. Linda once went through a period during which she designed and decorated glass bottles; one was lovelier than the next, and our home proudly displays many of them.

Linda is interested in various aspects of the supernatural. We have talked about this through the years. She knows I am a skeptic, and she called me one day to ask if I would come over to her apartment in Beverly Hills and take a look at a brochure she had been given.

The brochure was an advertisement for a weekend seminar on remote viewing. I had never heard the term *remote viewing* before, but as it turned out, I had actually read about a remote viewing experience in a science fiction novel written by the renowned author Arthur C. Clarke (the same guy who is responsible for Clarke's Law). *Childhood's End*[1] was certainly one of the best science fiction novels of the 1950s. It described the arrival on Earth of an alien species whose function was to oversee the coming evolution of humanity. In a chapter I vividly recalled, one of the first children to undergo the evolution had talks with a psychiatrist about dreams the child was having concerning different worlds. The psychiatrist discusses the different worlds the child describes with a member of the alien species; these worlds are known to the aliens but could not possibly be known to humans, who have yet to venture beyond the moon. The chapter is beautifully written, as is the entire novel; my memory of it was still vivid after nearly 50 years. This was clearly an instance of remote viewing, in which people see with their minds a place they have never seen or have heard described.

My visit to Linda's apartment took place shortly after we had invaded Iraq in 2003. The regime had been overthrown and Saddam Hussein had gone into hiding. Linda told me that the man who was running the remote-viewing seminar had been a former military officer connected with a top-secret project to locate Saddam Hussein via remote viewing. I recalled reading that the military had shown previous interest in extra-sensory perception. Although it struck me that the best this plan could produce was a lucky guess, it didn't appear to be something that would consume the billions of tax dollars invested in most military enterprises. After this discussion, Linda handed me the brochure. I looked at the front page and knew right away that the man was a charlatan.

The front page of the brochure was littered with mathematical symbols. This was before the television show *Numb3rs* became a hit, but even people with no formal training in advanced mathematics can recognize mathematical symbols, especially when there are numbers and equal signs all over the place. However, the symbols were incorrectly used and positioned—it was as if a child had been shown a page of advanced mathematics for three minutes, the page was then taken away, and the child was asked to write down what he remembered. Obviously, some symbols would be correctly remembered, but they would be written down erroneously juxtaposed with other correctly remembered and incorrectly remembered symbols in such a way that what was written made no sense. For example, a child who had never seen an arithmetic equation might look at "2+3=5" and recall it as being written "23T-5."

Okay, the front page of the brochure could have been the result of sloppy proofreading, but there were also serious errors in the description of mathematical objects and their uses; that's what raised the red flag. The brochure had the mathematical symbol $\delta(t)$ accurately labeled as the Dirac delta function (many mathematical constructs are named after the first person who used them), but described the function as having the values 0 and 1 with 0 representing nothingness and 1 representing creation. The Dirac delta function, according to the man who was conducting the seminar, therefore represented how creation proceeds from nothingness.

There are a lot of technical errors here. There is a function which takes the value 0 until a certain point in time, after which it takes the value 1, but it is the unit step function, sometimes called the Heaviside unit step function (also after the person who first used it). The Dirac delta function is also called an impulse function, and it is an unusual mathematical object. Imagine that you leave a 1-watt bulb on for 1 hour: you have used 1 watt-hour of energy. You would use the same amount of energy—1 watt-hour—if you left a 2-watt bulb on for 1/2 an hour, or a 10-watt bulb on for 1/10 of an hour, or a 100-watt bulb on for 1/100 of an hour, and so on. The Dirac delta function is a mathematical idealization of infinite power applied for an infinitesimal length of time in such a way that precisely 1 watt-hour of energy is used.

Additionally, 0 and 1 represent specific numerical values of something being measured. Anyone who uses 0 to depict nothingness and 1 to depict creation is going where no mathematician has gone before, and is either generations ahead of his or her time, or has completely lost it, or is trying to peddle snake oil. Considering that the weekend seminar in remote viewing cost a pretty penny, I had no hesitation in casting my vote for the latter.

I was very sure that the individual conducting this seminar was a con artist, or at the very least was trying to convince potential attendees that he had mathematical expertise when he really didn't. Nonetheless, Linda clearly was interested in attending, and it may well have proved to be an enjoyable experience. Lots of people go to Vegas knowing they will probably lose money gambling, but still do so because they enjoy the experience. As a result, I gave Linda the following advice: if this is something you want to do, treat it like a trip to Vegas. Budget accordingly, enjoy yourself, and don't expect to win. Although I'm absolutely convinced that the individual running this seminar was a con artist, I'm also convinced that a lot of people enjoy this type of thing. Once they know the risks, it's up to them to make the decision that's appropriate for them. As a libertarian, that's my attitude towards a lot of things.

An Enlightened Approach to Enlightenment

A statement that really resonates with me is "If only people weren't so busy righting wrongs, there wouldn't be so many wrongs to right."[2] I think the world would be a lot better off with fewer crusaders. The original Crusades were undertaken with the apparently noble motive of enlightenment—to bring the True Word of God to the heathens but some of the problems in the world today can be traced back to these endeavors. Enlightenment at the point of a sword is not an enlightened approach.

I think it's noble to enlighten—after all, that's the role of a teacher, my chosen profession—but once you have enlightened, it's time to step back and allow the now-enlightened individual freedom of choice. Enlighten, but don't encroach. However, there are limits to freedom of choice, and someone should step in when an individual makes choices that are potentially harmful to others, especially those who cannot protect themselves. For example, we don't allow parents or guardians to deprive their charges of adequate medical care because of their religious beliefs. We do allow parents to home-school their children and teach creationism, though, because if there is a danger in doing so, it's nowhere near as serious as preventing the child from having a blood transfusion when the child desperately needs one.

In addition to limits, there are boundaries. Despite the fact that there are a few individuals espousing "creation science," the overwhelming majority of the scientific community sees creationism as unscientific. The scientific community gets to decide what is science and what isn't. There are lots of places where the Biblical story of creation can be taught—but a science class isn't one of them. I think most scientists feel the same way that I do. You aren't allowed to represent yourself as a policeman or a doctor if you aren't one; and you shouldn't be allowed to label a field of study as a science when it isn't.

Why not? Because it's the intellectual and educational equivalent of false advertising. You're not allowed to claim that a product will do something it won't or is something that it isn't. That goes for intellectual products as well as physical ones.

I live in Redondo Beach, California. Within 3 miles of where I live, there are at least three long-established psychics. I say "long-established" because I know their places of business have been in existence for more than a decade. I would certainly not advise anyone I know to consult them, but they do not advertise themselves as scientists. The dictionary defines *psychic* as one who is allegedly sensitive to psychic influences, and I have no bone to pick with them because they do not claim that what they are doing is scientific. But I can certainly find bones to pick for this reason. Here's one.

Numerology: the 2,500-Year-Old "Science"?

Sometime in the mid-1980s I went to a party. The hostess was functioning as a good hostess should, introducing the guests to each other, and she was in the process of introducing me to Judy, a vivacious young musician. "Judy," she said, "I'd like you to meet Jim. He's a mathematician."

Never before, and never since, had a vivacious young lady reacted to being introduced to me as Judy did. Her eyes opened wide, she smiled, and said words I had never heard before, "I've ALWAYS wanted to meet a mathematician."

Generally, *nobody* wants to meet a mathematician—and you can probably guess the reason why. Mathematicians remind them of their experiences with mathematics in school, which were generally uncomfortable. I read an article a number of years ago that I enjoyed, but winced when I read a line in it which said that artists were interesting people with uninteresting ideas, and scientists were uninteresting people with interesting ideas. I would argue otherwise, but I think a lot of people would agree with it—at least the part about scientists being uninteresting people.

I was able to savor the novelty of a vivacious young lady actually wanting to meet a mathematician for approximately two seconds. Judy's next sentence was, "Tell me, just why is nine the master number?" Although I had not been exposed to any of the tenets of numerology, it was clear that Judy wanted to meet a numerologist rather than a mathematician. I suspect that for every one person who would like to meet a mathematician, there are a lot more who would enjoy meeting a numerologist.

Numerology is sometimes described as the 2,500-year-old science of numbers. Being described as a science (it's not) induces people to believe that it is a branch of knowledge (it's actually a branch of belief). Because it's 2,500 years old, people believe that it's venerable knowledge. It's certainly venerable, in the sense of having been around a long time. The fact that it deals with numbers adds an aura of authenticity; after all, there's a book in the Bible called Numbers, and numbers are felt by many—including scientists—to be the language of the Universe.

Many years ago I saw a lecture given by Linus Pauling, one of the most famous scientists of the 20th century, at a college campus. There was a question-and-answer session after the lecture, during which a student asked Pauling what he thought of astrology. Pauling took a few seconds to formulate his reply, and then told the student that astrology was developed by Ptolemy, undoubtedly one of the most brilliant men of his era. However, in constructing the principles of astrology, Ptolemy had to rely upon the knowledge that had been gathered at that time, and that knowledge was sadly deficient. Pauling felt that Ptolemy, had he been around today, would realize that knowledge gained since his time rendered astrology inadequate to the task of describing the Universe.

Ptolemy, however, lived after the birth of Christ—not 2,500 years ago, when numerology presumably was created, and lived in a much more intellectually and scientifically sophisticated world than the world of ancient Greece. Consider some aspects of the world 2,500 years ago, approximately 500 years before the birth of Christ. Science, such as it was, was amazingly primitive. Even such elementary theories as the four elements (earth, air, fire, water) and the four humors (black bile, yellow bile, phlegm, and blood) had yet to be fully developed. True, there were occasional impressive achievements by various cultures, but considering the relative development of medicine, I'd rather be very sick now than slightly sick in 500 BC. Infections were liable to be fatal, practically any injury could prove to be permanently disabling, and life really was nasty, brutish, and short. And you'd like me to believe that these cultures had developed a brilliant method for analyzing personality and predicting the future, when they had virtually nothing resembling any aspect of modern science or technology? Sorry, I'm just not capable of doing that.

I said a few paragraphs ago that numerology was not a science. One of the reasons that I made that statement is because every science known to man advances with the passage of time. Just look at the achievements of the last century in the natural sciences. To list only a few, biologists have deciphered the genetic code, astronomers have traced the beginning of the Universe to a Big Bang, physicists have pieced together a model which describes matter and forces, and chemists have created a vast array of synthetics which equal or outdo much of what is produced by the natural world. Meteorologists are able to produce much more accurate forecasts extending further into the future, geologists understand the forces that create earthquakes and are making strides to be able to predict them—and that's just the natural sciences. Advances have likewise been made in the major social sciences as well; they're just not as startling, because the social sciences started later than the natural sciences and have to overcome the difficulty of not being able to measure as accurately or produce controlled experiments.

The advent of computers has created entirely new sciences. The word *bioinformatics* has only been in existence for a couple of decades, but now you can get college degrees—and, more importantly, high-paying jobs—in it. Computers have been integrated into every one of the natural and social sciences. Not only do computers store and process data, but they can be used to test all sorts of hypotheses and simulate a large number of physical processes. Airplane and automobile design are now largely done on computers, and without computers many of the recent advances in our understanding of the physical Universe could never have been made.

Speaking of "recent advances," try searching the Internet for "recent advances" in the sciences. There are thousands of pages of references for recent advances in physics, recent advances in chemistry, recent advances in biology—the list goes on and on for every one of the sciences. Now try "recent advances" in astrology. The first page of a Google search refers to a book on natal astrology written in 1977, and a report in a journal in 1978. The pickings are equally slim if you try "recent advances" in numerology. It's hard to apply the term "science" to a field of knowledge that makes no advances. Art, music, and literature are certainly not sciences, yet even they make advances. Philosophy, also not classified as a science, is an extremely dynamic field. Yet numerology and astrology are totally static. The only fields with which I am familiar that are equally static are religions; the writings upon which religions are founded were generally written a long time ago. Although interpretations of religions change, the religions—and the core writings on which they are based—advance at glacial speed, if they advance at all. In this respect, numerology and astrology resemble religions much more closely than they resemble sciences.

There are also a number of very puzzling aspects to numerology, which render it considerably less credible—at least to me. One idea which permeated several of the sites I looked at is something called the lifepath number. I was born on August 29, 1941—my lifepath number is computed by adding the digits when the date of my birth is written 8/29/1941 and reducing them until a single digit number remains. Adding up the digits, 8+2+9+1+9+4+1 = 34. Adding up the digits again, 3+4 = 7. This is my lifepath number. Sevens are cerebral loners who appreciate natural beauty. If they lack faith, they become cynical and turn to some form of escape. They do not want to reveal their inner selves.

Hmm, two out of five. I'm certainly cerebral, but I'm very gregarious. I appreciate natural beauty—but then, who doesn't? I have faith in certain things (the value of the American constitution, Euclidean geometry, and the Laws of Thermodynamics), but not in others. However, I am far from being a cynic, whom Oscar Wilde once described as a man who knows the price of everything and the value of nothing.[3] My inner self is pretty much my outer self, and it's on display, for better or worse, to everyone I meet.

Let me point out a couple of the obvious problems I have with numerology—why, even in the absence of formal testing, it makes no sense to me. If numerology is 2,500 years old, why are its key numbers computed using the decimal system (which didn't achieve its full prominence until the Hindus invented the number zero, which many historians feel occurred well after the birth of Christ)? Maybe this is the best numerology can summon up in the way of a "recent advance." Why is the Gregorian calendar, adopted in 1582, the one that is used—why not the Hebrew calendar, which is substantially older? Finally, the Gregorian calendar was modified in 1582 by eliminating 10 days. This was done by mandating that the day after October 4, 1582 was denoted October 15, 1582. I don't know what effect this has on numerology in general, but it sure plays havoc with your lifepath number.

I feel roughly the same about numerology and astrology that I do about remote-viewing seminars. People can find all sorts of entertainment in these things, and it's a grim world sometimes, so any form of entertainment that is not harmful can be something worth pursuing. That's the libertarian in me. If you want to have fun with numerology, go right ahead; there's a lot of nonsense in the world and a lot of it provides entertainment and distraction from the troubles of life. Maybe for some people numerology is like that. Soccer is an enjoyable distraction for many people, yet soccer riots have killed hundreds, maybe thousands, of people throughout the world. I haven't heard of any numerology riots or astrology riots.

However, to quote Stevie Wonder, when you believe in things that you don't understand, then you suffer.[4] You really suffer when *nobody* understands them, because there's nothing to understand. I have nothing against reading and enjoying your horoscope; many astrology columns nowadays include a disclaimer that it is intended as entertainment. If you want to make decisions for yourself based on your horoscope, that's your lookout. But if you start using it to make decisions for others (as Nancy Reagan did when scheduling presidential appointments for her husband), my feeling is that not only do you believe in things that you don't understand, you may be causing someone else to suffer in consequence. That's wrong, and that's one of the big reasons I feel people should make an effort to know the truth. There's a known connection between smoking and lung cancer, but if you know the risks and choose to smoke, I'm certainly not going to try to stop you. There's also a known connection between secondhand smoke and lung cancer, and so if you're going to smoke, I feel you have an obligation to do so where you don't run the risk of hurting others.

There's a side effect of numerology that also bothers me. There are millions of people who are utterly fascinated by numbers—obviously people who spend time with numerology can be counted among these. If only these people had turned their fascination with numbers into learning something useful, they'd be a lot better off (with the exception of those few individuals who have managed to make a living by supplying numerology entertainment to others). There's a pretty good chance they'd have managed to produce something from which we all could benefit. Show me a million people who are fascinated by numbers, and the law of averages tells you that some of them have the capacity to be damned good mathematicians, scientists, and engineers.

The Truth About Numbers

Don't get me wrong—numbers and numerical patterns do convey something about the Universe as well. There are some intriguing numerical patterns associated with the periodic table of the elements. For instance, the number of electrons in totally filled shells ascend according to the pattern 2, 6, 10, 14.... The columnar arrangement of the periodic table shows that many elements, such as noble gases (helium, xenon, krypton) or alkali metals (lithium, potassium, sodium, calcium) have many properties in common. These numerical patterns have a tremendous influence on our lives, but they don't display their effects because of the numbers, but because of the scientific properties that involve these numbers. The number 8, for example, is felt to be extremely lucky in many oriental cultures, and in a sense it is; we're all here because of the number 8. Oxygen, so vital for animal life, has atomic number 8.

Numbers and the End of the World

You may have missed it, but May 21, 2011 was the end of the world. At least, that's what Harold Camping, a Biblical scholar with a BS degree in civil engineering from the University of California at Berkeley, predicted, based on his interpretation of the numbers in the Bible. I recall clicking on a Web publication which offered two infallible numerical proofs, using Biblical information, that May 21, 2011 would mark the end of the world. This was the same Harold Camping who had twice gone to bat with a similar prediction for May 21, 1988, and September 6, 1994. Obviously, he struck out both times. Yet, according to what I read, he had received more than $37 million in donations to his Church.

When May 21, 2011 came and went—and most of us were still here—Camping revised his prediction. May 21 now marked the first day of the Period of Judgment, during which we would all be assessed as to who would be allowed to enter the kingdom of the righteous. The new, revised, absolutely correct end of the world was now to be October 21, 2011.

There's a great temptation to resort to sarcasm here—especially for someone raised in New York, as I was—but you have to feel sorry for people who genuinely believed this stuff. You have to feel even sorrier for people who wrecked their lives on the basis of this prediction, because there were some who sold all their possessions, quit their jobs, and went to join Camping to await the Rapture.

This particular prediction—or two predictions—received so much coverage that you'd think this was the end of the End of the World predictions. No, looming ahead of us is the real, honest-to-goodness End of the World, as predicted by the Mayan calendar. That's going to happen on December 21, 2012.

Consider this—a recent poll showed that one person in seven believes that the world will end within their lifetime.[5] Okay, that's pretty startling, but even more amazing is that 10 percent of the people believe that the world will end in 2012—because that's what the Mayan calendar says. And how could the Mayans be wrong about something so important?

I'm writing this in May 2012, and I've already bought tickets for several events that will take place in 2013, so you can be sure where I'm placing my bet. The world will still be here in 2013, and 20,013, and 200,013, and 2,000,013, and 20,000,013, and 200,000,013. But it's going to start getting hot about then, because the Sun is going to start to heat up, so I'm not so sure about 2,000,000,013.

Crystals, Pentagrams, and the Like

Because geometry has been around as long as arithmetic, there is also a tradition of believing that geometrical shapes and patterns convey something deep about the Universe. In a sense this is true; but once again, it is not some intrinsic property of a particular shape but the connection between that shape and physical or chemical function.

Circles, for instance, are in a sense perfect shapes—so perfect that many attempts were made to construct astronomical theories based on the fact that something so perfect as a circle must manifest itself in the behavior of the heavenly bodies. Ptolemy, indisputably one of the brightest men of his era, constructed a "theory of epicycles"—circles superimposed upon circles, to explain the apparent motion of the planets. Even as late as the early 17th century, Johannes Kepler attempted to explain the orbits of the planets as circles with the Sun at the center. It didn't work; the actual orbits are ellipses, and the explanation of precisely why this is the case is one of the great triumphs of Newton's Theory of Universal Gravitation.

Crystals are, indeed, one of Nature's most beautiful creations. They incorporate the beauty of geometry with the precisely-structured requirements of physics and chemistry. I have fond memories of when I performed a chemistry experiment that consisted of "growing" a beautiful blue copper sulfate crystal. However, the "mystic crystal revelation" referred to in the wonderful song *Aquarius*,[6] which ushered in the 1970s, is unknown to science. There is absolutely no evidence that crystals do anything other than what they are intended to do by the laws of chemistry and physics. Oh, yes, their beauty and rarity prompts people to pay large sums of money for them, but there's nothing mystic about that. Both beauty and rarity have economic value.

Lastly, the less said about pentagrams, the better. If you live in Carl Sagan's demon-haunted world, and you believe that pentagrams either have some special appeal for demons or protect you somehow from them (I know they're supposed to do one or the other, but don't know which and don't intend to find out), you inhabit a world that was left behind with the Salem witch trials. It makes for fun entertainment—I happily confess that I enjoyed episodes of *Buffy the Vampire Slayer* and *Charmed*—but a lot of entertainment is based on the willing suspension of disbelief. Be entertained by it, but don't be guided by it.

Of course, lots of us believe in things we don't understand. I don't understand how my car works—except in a general sort of way—and that goes for most of the machinery that makes life comfortable. However, there are people who understand cars, and other machines, perfectly. No one understands astrology or numerology anywhere near as well as a good mechanic understands cars—because there isn't anything there to understand. Astrology and numerology have rules governing the interpretation of phenomena (birthdates for astrology, lifepath numbers for numerology) which have been passed down from practitioner to practitioner, which may very well have worked in a few instances. After all, the proverbial stopped clock is right twice a day. Astrology and numerology are basically fortune-telling devices and have no causal connection to any of the principles known to govern the Universe.

Let's go back for a moment to the idea that facts fall into three categories: the known, the unknown, and the unknowable. Numerology and astrology just don't fit in very well with known facts; I've shown some of this and will present more later. Unless science grinds to a complete halt, there are unknown facts which we will discover later. Could numerology and astrology fit in with these unknown facts?

Of course, that's what a lot of purveyors of astrological and numerological materials want you to believe. They often claim that astrology and numerology (among others) reveal secrets that transcend what science currently knows. Could this be the case? Are there discoveries waiting to be made which could validate these claims? Going even further, are there unknowable principles that science can never know, but which fit right in with numerology and astrology? In order to get a handle on these questions, we need to examine what science knows and how it knows that it knows it.

3 The Search for Truth

The search for truth is one of the abiding preoccupations of the human race, and has been for as long as there have been written records of our activities. The search for truth takes place in different areas, in philosophy and religion just as much as science and mathematics. Those who believe in the reality of supernatural and paranormal phenomena are often just as earnest in their search for truth as those who search for truth in science and mathematics.

One of the more successful TV shows dealing with the supernatural and the paranormal was *The X-Files*, a series which enjoyed a lengthy run from 1993 to 2002. The opening catchphrase for the show was "The truth is out there... somewhere." Agents Scully and Mulder, the show's continuing protagonists, were every bit as involved in trying to ascertain the truth as the most diligent scientific researcher. The show obviously struck a responsive chord with a sizeable audience, and certainly no TV show on either real or hypothetical scientific research has done as well. One might say that the *Star Trek* series, which has appeared on TV in several different incarnations for almost 50 years, at least has some background in science, but the appeal of *Star Trek* is in its characters and stories, not in its science. I think it is fair to say that the search for the truth played a much greater role in the appeal of the *X-Files* than in the appeal of *Star Trek*, because scientific truth is generally nowhere near as titillating to the vast majority of people as are the possibilities of mysterious truth inherent in the supernatural and the paranormal.

Nonetheless, science has been far more successful in improving our daily lives than have the efforts to find whatever supernatural or paranormal truth may be out there. So has mathematics. So let's look at how the search for truth is conducted in these two areas and where this search has met with substantial success.

How Math and Science Get Vetted

Mathematicians and scientists are just as capable of making errors as other people. What distinguishes mathematics and science is that truth is established in mathematics by logical argument, and truth is established in science by experimental verification. This means that truth can be verified independently of those who first propound a supposed truth. There are practical problems with this in both areas. Most mathematicians prefer to work on their own research and check the work of others only when it directly impinges on theirs. Sometimes, subtle errors of logic may go undetected—the Four Color Problem (any map can be colored using only four colors in such a way that no two countries which share a common boundary have the same color) provides a famous example of a theorem that was believed to have been proven for more than a decade before an error was detected.

Math and science are both vetted in the same way, through refereeing. A mathematician who believes he has made a worthwhile contribution writes up his results and sends his paper to a journal.

The editor of the journal sends it to a referee—an established mathematician who has published papers in the same field as the paper being refereed. The referee checks the paper for both accuracy and importance. There is a classic rejection letter—possibly apocryphal—which stated, "This paper contains many new and interesting results. Regrettably, the new results are not interesting, and the interesting results are not new." If a paper is rejected, the referee may suggest improvements which would render the paper publishable. Occasionally, a paper that is rejected by one journal may be submitted to another and accepted; in this case, the paper was probably accepted because the second referee felt the results were a more significant contribution than did the first.

Scientific papers may be either theoretical or experimental. Theoretical papers are vetted in much the same way as mathematical papers. However, often competing explanations are published as possible explanations in the hope that someone will figure out a way of deciding which of the explanations is correct. One well-known conflict took place in the middle of the 20th century, between the Big Bang and Continuous Creation theories of cosmology. The Big Bang theory postulated that the Universe originated in a giant explosion (the "Big Bang"), a single moment at which all matter was created. The Continuous Creation theory hypothesized that the creation of matter was an ongoing process. Papers on both theories were published, as long as it was an open question as to which theory was correct, but in the end an experiment was performed which obtained results that could only be accounted for by the Big Bang theory. After that, no more papers were published on Continuous Creation—at least in research journals, although it shows up in histories of science or in books such as this one.

Papers describing experimental results are treated differently from theoretical papers. Ideally, a scientific experiment should be reproducible, but it may cost too much to duplicate a large experiment, or there may be only one facility capable of performing it. As a result, it may be impossible to show initially that an error has been made. Nonetheless, errors will eventually surface, indirectly if not directly, because other experiments constructed on false premises will yield incorrect or inexplicable results, and if this happens with some consistency, the error will be tracked down. Most instances of scientific fraud are detected this way.

Defining What Is Meant by "Supernatural"

I believe that the explanation I will present for the possibility of supernatural or paranormal phenomena is a credible one. However, it does rely on hypotheses which, although believed by a large number of scientists, have not yet been substantiated.

I said in the Introduction that I believe that mathematics and science open a "rational window" that not only permits supernatural phenomena to exist, but requires it. I started writing a previous book having no belief in reincarnation, remote viewing, ghosts, or UFOs, and nothing I have learned or believe I have learned has changed my position. There is no contradiction (at least that I can see) between those two statements, and that is largely because of the definition I am using of what constitutes supernatural phenomena. Definitions are extremely important: we've got to agree what we are talking about. So let's look at what the dictionary has to say about the word *supernatural.*

How should we define the term *supernatural* in order to have a legitimate shot at reaching a conclusion about the existence or nonexistence of supernatural phenomena? The online Merriam-Webster dictionary gives two definitions.[1]

The first is "of or relating to an order of existence beyond the visible observable universe; especially: of or relating to God or a god, demigod, spirit, or devil." This definition splits into two parts. "Relating to an order of existence beyond the visible observable universe" gives us the hope that there are things we can tackle, because we can at least get some idea of what constitutes the visible observable Universe.

To the scientist, "visible" and "observable" are very different terms. Visible light is confined to a very narrow portion of the electromagnetic spectrum. There are numerous depictions of the electromagnetic spectrum, but most are logarithmic in nature. The distance on the chart from wavelengths of 1 to 100 meters, a range of 2 orders of magnitude, is the same as the distance on the chart from wavelengths of .0001 (10^{-4}) meters to .01 (10^{-2}) meters, also a range of 2 orders of magnitude. The logarithmic presentation of the chart is necessary because electromagnetic radiation has wavelengths from the almost ridiculously short gamma rays—about .000000000000000001 meters—to long radio waves, such as are found in AM radio, and those can be more than 10,000 meters long. The visible portion of the spectrum occupies an extremely small portion of the total extent of the electromagnetic spectrum.

Science, however, does not confine "observable" to "visible," which is fortunate for any workable definition of supernatural phenomena. If we were stuck with the visible, electrons, bacteria, radio, and X-rays would be considered supernatural phenomena—and at one point some of these were indeed considered to be supernatural. The advance of science pushes back the domain of the supernatural. However, the second part of the definition, which deals with gods and spirits, is simply out of bounds for science. Science needs something it can measure or observe, and while science doesn't say that gods and spirits can't exist, they haven't been shown to be observable or measurable. Nor is the idea of a god or a spirit something that can be falsified.

Laws of Nature

The second definition, "departing from what is usual or normal especially so as to appear to transcend the laws of nature" is something science can sink its teeth into. Science, after all, deals with laws of Nature. Admittedly, the term *law of Nature* is also subject to some interpretation. Centuries ago, the birth of a two-headed animal was seen as an abomination, certainly a violation of the laws of Nature as they were understood at the time, and possibly an event auguring something exceptional that would happen in the future. We now understand that the laws of Nature encompass birth anomalies because of defects in the replication process, and the birth of a two-headed animal merely gets added to the catalogue of such creatures.

On a recent trip to Taiwan, I visited a beautiful Buddhist temple on the outskirts of Sun Moon Lake, the summer home of former Premier and Madame Chiang-Kai Shek. The temple had a picture of a woman who had been born with a second face, complete with functioning mouth, on the upper right side of her head. One can only imagine what would have happened to this woman if this had occurred in Salem, Massachusetts, during the time of the witch trials. It is a tribute to this woman's strength of character when presented with what almost all of us would conceive of as substantial adversity. She took her appearance as a message that she was to devote her life to the mission of spreading the Buddhist religion.

There is a clear message for us: just because something qualifies as unusual or bizarre does not mean that it is proof of the existence of paranormal or supernatural phenomena. The laws of genetics are clear, and the woman referred to in the previous paragraph did not arise as the result of some overturning of the laws of Nature. Conjoined twins have long been recognized as a natural occurrence, even before the exact mechanism of the development of human being from fertilized cell was elucidated in its entirety.

While certainly a much rarer occurrence than conjoined twins, a person with two physical faces is a natural rather than a supernatural phenomenon.

Part of the mission of science is to determine what the natural laws are. Some of the natural laws, such as the Law (or Theory) of Universal Gravitation, can be phrased mathematically. Some, such as the cell theory, are more qualitative in nature. The cell theory says that cells are the fundamental unit of structure, function, and organization in living things, and that new cells are formed from other cells.

While the cell theory lacks the predictive power of the Law of Universal Gravitation, it is almost certainly the more valuable theory from the standpoint of the well-being of humanity. The cell theory is one of the reasons that we no longer believe in spontaneous generation—the appearance of living organisms from out of nowhere—and led to the germ theory of disease, which has resulted in a rational approach to the control of diseases. No one would question that antibiotics are a better treatment for bacterial diseases than attempts to rid the body of evil spirits through incantations.

In general, the more complicated an object, the harder it is to understand. A galaxy contains hundreds of billions of stars which interact with each other gravitationally, electrically, and magnetically. In addition, there are gas clouds, planets, and maybe black holes, but nonetheless we understand the behavior of a galaxy far better than we understand the behavior of a single living cell.

Not knowing the complete set of natural laws that govern cells and the aggregations of cells that form individual beings, we have yet to push the boundary between natural and supernatural in the area of living entities anywhere near as far back as we have in the physical sciences. As a result, many of the candidates for supernatural phenomena that attract attention involve living or formerly living entities.

A good informal definition of *supernatural*, and one that would be accepted by many people, is the idea that the supernatural is something that cannot be explained by science. The key word here is "cannot." As we have noted, there are numerous phenomena to which previous generations undoubtedly affixed the label of supernatural which now fall into the realm of everyday experience. Of those currently alive, only someone completely uneducated is unaware that germs cause disease, and practically everyone on Earth has heard the voices from beyond that constitute radio broadcasts. Ghosts are supernatural to us, as they certainly would have been to someone in the 15th century, but television would have been supernatural to a visitor from that century, because it transcended the natural laws as that visitor knew them. As a result, what is felt to be supernatural tends to recede with the advance of science. Yesterday's supernatural often becomes today's commonplace science or technology. This presents a problem in defining the supernatural which has been recognized for some time.

Are Ghosts Supernatural? Tales of the Ghost Hunters

Let's consider the problem of whether ghosts constitute a supernatural phenomenon. There are two major objections to this. The first is that there are no rigorously documented and authenticated occurrences of ghosts. One of the books I consulted while writing is *From Shaman to Scientist: Essays on Humanity's Search for Spirits.*[2] In the foreword, Richard Wiseman describes an attempt to find ghosts via scientific means in allegedly haunted vaults in Edinburgh, Scotland. I chuckled as I read this, recalling an amusing episode in the wonderful 1960s TV Series *The Avengers*, in which two teams representing the organizations F.O.G. (Friends of Ghosts) and S.M.O.G. (Scientific Measurement of Ghosts) embarked upon a similar quest—and in a similar environment. Wiseman concludes that although they found no evidence of ghosts, they learned a lot of value about people's reactions during these investigations.

Let's concentrate on the part in which Wiseman mentions that they employed equipment to monitor a wide range of environmental variables. Any believer in ghosts can immediately account for the failure of the team to detect ghosts in two ways. The first is obvious: they did not employ the right ghost detection equipment. Maybe they should have consulted the writers of the film *Ghostbusters* to make sure they were properly accessorized, or they could merely have browsed online (possibly harder in 2001 than now) for paranormal ghost detection equipment, which is readily available for purchase.

The second objection would be that—duh!—a ghost is not detectable by means known to science. Not science now, not science ever. But how, then, do people become aware of ghosts? That, too, is obvious: they possess senses for phenomena that science cannot duplicate. But how can we be sure of that? Assuming that we eventually find evidence of genuine "ghosts," this evidence is a part of the Universe as we know it and is no longer supernatural.

The formulation and acceptance by the scientific community of a natural law tells us we really understand something. We may understand it in a qualitative sense, such as the cell theory, or we may understand it quantitatively and operationally, such as the Theory of Universal Gravitation. Nobody, scientist or otherwise, would have a problem describing either the cell theory or the Theory of Universal Gravitation as a natural law. We don't require a natural law to be complete or completely accurate; we just require it to describe some aspect of Nature and do a really good and verifiable job of it.

There was a time, before Isaac Newton, that we did not know the algebraic form that the Law of Universal Gravitation took.

Nonetheless, we did know certain things about gravitation. Everyone knew that when you drop a rock, it falls down towards the Earth, rather than up towards the sky, or sideways. Everyone knew that rocks dropped from a greater height hit the ground harder than rocks dropped from a lesser height. Everyone knew that although you could certainly survive having a pillow dropped on your head from a height of five feet, the same could not be said if a 2-ton weight were dropped on your head from the same height. All these observations were made without knowing the exact form of the Law of Gravitation. It is not clear if the Egyptians or the Greeks ever considered the possibility of discovering a Law of Gravitation, but they certainly knew that gravity was a real phenomenon.

But what if there were a relationship between the measurable parameters involved in the Law of Gravitation which *did* exist, much like the Law of Gravitation, but which could *not* be deduced by science? Such a relationship would certainly have the attribute that it was a phenomenon that science could not explain.

This appears to be a catch-22 type situation. How would we know that there was such a relationship? Wouldn't we have to do some observing and measuring in order to confirm it? And, in so doing, aren't we starting down the same road that led to Newton's Theory of Universal Gravitation, which Galileo took when he started measuring the velocities of balls rolling down inclined planes? And even if we were not sufficiently bright ourselves to be able to put together our observations and measurements in some sort of relationship, how can we be sure that future generations, armed with better technologies and better theoretical tools, might not be able to do so?

You would undoubtedly be justified in wondering how we could be certain that a relationship we could never know could even exist. However, let's suppose for the moment that we could be certain that such a relationship could exist. Part of what I am going to do in this book is to try to convince you that, even though we might not be able to ever find such a relationship, we could know for certain that it would have to exist. If I can convince you of this, such a relationship would certainly fall into the "supernatural" category, at least in terms of the definition of the word "supernatural" that I am using. It would be a part of the Universe that is hidden to both the probing instruments of science and the mathematical and logical explorations that are an essential part of the scientific toolbox.

This would be, to some extent, what many people consider to be supernatural. It's a truth that would be out there—somewhere—but not a truth that we could ever know. Search though they might, Mulder and Scully would never find it—nor could anyone else. In addition to the idea that this is something that cannot be explained by science, it would be something that fit into a pattern which forever remains hidden. That's certainly mysterious and exotic, and gets to the heart of what a lot of people consider to be the essence of supernatural phenomena.

Types of Supernatural Phenomena

There are a large number of possible supernatural phenomena, but there are some which are directly related to our understanding of ordinary ("normal") human capabilities. Some of these involve phenomena which go beyond our understanding of the limits of human sensory capability, such as remote viewing (as discussed in Chapter 2). Some of these involve phenomena which go beyond our understanding of the limits of what the mind can do. A good example of this is psychokinesis; the ability to directly influence the physical world using only the mind. Finally, some of these involve a world that is currently not accessible to the instruments which we use to obtain measurements. This latter example goes to the core of what science is and what it can do.

What Is Science?

Having come up with a usable definition of what the word "supernatural" means, let's look at what science is—especially because many people intuitively feel that the supernatural "is" what science "is not." Two definitions of science that I found satisfactory are "a branch of knowledge or study dealing with a body of facts or truths systematically arranged and showing the operation of general laws," and "systematic knowledge of the physical or material world gained through observation and experimentation."[3]

There are two types of observations: qualitative and quantitative. Although some of what constitutes science proceeds on the basis of qualitative observations, science has a strong preference for quantitative observations, because these can be independently confirmed much more easily than qualitative ones. One of the difficulties we encounter in dealing with personal anecdotal experiences is that it is difficult to impossible to confirm these quantitatively.

First of all, there is the difficulty that independent observers may not even agree upon the observation from a qualitative standpoint. Consider how this affects the perception of sensory information. Some sensory information is reasonably well quantified; for instance, middle C on the piano is a vibration with a measurable frequency of 256 cycles per second. Any reasonably competent musician can identify when middle C is being played, and people with perfect pitch can detect whether the frequency of the vibration differs from 256 cycles per second by an extremely small amount. That quantifies what middle C is, but just because we can detect it and musicians can label it with reasonable accuracy, is the experience of hearing middle C the same for everyone? Or seeing the color blue?

Taste is a lot more subtle and difficult to quantify than sight and sound. I'm not sure what would be the culinary equivalent of middle C; for the purposes of this discussion, let's just use a food that almost everyone has tasted, corn flakes. I've chosen corn flakes because it really doesn't matter which manufacturer produces it, corn flakes taste just about the same (at least to me)—unlike pizza, which comes in a wide number of varieties. Some people like corn flakes, some don't. Obviously the sensory experience of corn flakes differs from person to person. If we choose something such as asparagus, the variation is incredibly wide: some people love asparagus; some hate it. You might be able to say to someone that you prefer asparagus to spinach; you might even be able to say that you prefer asparagus to corn flakes, but how do you convey this experience to others?

Does that mean that science is doomed when it comes to discussing mental experience? Well, we haven't figured out how to do it yet, but that doesn't mean we'll never figure it out.

There's an important difference between the two definitions of science given above. The first deals with patterns of arrangement and general laws, and the second talks about the physical or material world. Although people who believe strongly in supernatural or paranormal phenomena might say that there are general laws governing them which we have not yet discovered, the second definition's emphasis on the physical or material world immediately places it in opposition to the conventional idea of the environment in which supernatural and paranormal phenomena most frequently appear. Let's take a look at one of the most pervasive concepts in the world of the paranormal; the idea of spirit.

This isn't something that's easy to define. The first definition of spirit[4] in Merriam-Webster is "an animating or vital principle held to give life to physical organisms." There are clearly several problems with this definition. The simplest life form that we know of is a virus, in the sense that its genome is the smallest, and I don't think that the most ardent champion of the idea of spirit would spend a nanosecond defending the idea that a virus has a spirit. Even more complicated organisms lack a spirit; it's hard to say where to draw the line if there is a line to be drawn.

"Spirit" differs from "supernatural being or essence." How would you go about measuring "a supernatural being or essence"? There are actually two different things being discussed here. A supernatural being is usually thought of as a god or one of Carl Sagan's demons. It may be quintessentially good, as is postulated by many religions. It may be evil incarnate, also as postulated by many religions. A supernatural essence may be thought of as an ineffable quality that contributes to our humanity, often referred to as *soul.*

Can a supernatural being or essence be analyzed by science? That's not the type of thing that science deals with, no matter which definition of science is being used. Any nonphysical entity is inherently not quantifiable, and therefore no hypothesis concerning it can be tested.

Is it possible for something such as a soul to be a physical entity which, as of yet, has not been successfully measured but could conceivably persist after death in some physical way? Such a question might be anathema to someone who sees the soul as a genuine entity divorced from physical reality, but all the scientist has at the moment to work with are things you can measure. There are phenomena called solitons, which are packets of energy that persist unless they interact with their surroundings. Ball lightning is a good example of this; it's just a mass of electric charge. However, that's a long way from what is conventionally thought of as a soul.

Transcending the Laws of Nature

We have an intuitive understanding of what it means to transcend the laws of Nature—at least, insofar as we currently understand those laws. We also understand, whether we are scientists or not, that the laws of Nature have been revised in the past and may be in the future. Certainly, reincarnation, remote viewing, and ghosts transcend the laws of Nature; UFOs may or may not, depending on how long it takes them to get here. However, these are not the only phenomena which may transcend the laws of Nature. In fact, in order to decide what is meant by the phrase "transcend the laws of Nature," a mathematician would ask the following questions:

1. What are the laws of Nature?
2. What do we mean by transcending them?

Mathematics and science are extraordinarily successful disciplines in part because their definitions are so exact. Put 20 mathematicians in a room and ask them to define any mathematical concept, such as a triangle (or the Dirac delta function, which we discussed earlier), and you will get 20 identical or logically equivalent definitions. Put 20 psychologists in a room and ask them to define love or anxiety, and you will probably get several somewhat different definitions according to the schools of psychology to which the individual psychologists adhere.

I'm a mathematician. I intend to rigorously define what is meant by the laws of Nature, what is meant by transcending them, and show that there are reasonable assumptions under which phenomena which transcend the laws of Nature must exist. However, mathematics should also be useful. That's my opinion, but there are mathematicians who study mathematical objects which are defined by possessing a set of properties, even though currently no examples of such objects are known to exist. If I were to define natural laws so narrowly that there were virtually no natural laws, then supernatural phenomena would be the rule rather than the exception. This book would then be a fraud.

I am virtually certain that most scientists and non-scientists will agree with how I shall define natural laws. There may be some disagreement about what is meant by transcending them, and I think there will also be some disagreement about the circumstances that are required for natural laws to be transcended. We are, after all, talking about things that are nowhere near as precisely defined as triangles or Dirac delta functions, and encounter some of the same difficulties psychologists do when trying to discuss love. However, there is enough common ground among psychological theories that even though the specifics differ, everyone "knows" what love is.

Standards of Proof

The philosopher Karl Popper established falsifiability as the fundamental criterion for determining what is, and what is not, science. For a result to be scientific, it must be possible to be proven wrong. That is why creationism is not taught, and should not be taught, in science classes. The argument that life was divinely created is not something that can be proved false, and it is certainly not something that has been proven true.

In general, specific instances of what is deemed to be supernatural are not falsifiable. Ghosts, if they exist, are supernatural, at least according to our current understanding of natural laws. However, there is currently no scientific framework in which one can prove that there is no such thing as a ghost. Incidentally, if and when a fully documented and rigorously verifiable instance of a ghost is discovered, ghosts will move from the supernatural to the natural, because they will be part of the Universe as we know it. Many non-scientists feel that scientists refuse to admit the possibility of ghosts because their conception of the Universe is too narrow to include them. My guess is that the moment that ghosts become natural phenomena, entire branches of science will be developed to study them, because there is nothing that excites scientists more than genuinely new phenomena—as long as the new phenomena are genuine.

Nightfall 4

The previous chapters should make it clear that the task this book is undertaking is not an easy one to accomplish, if for no other reason than the job of establishing what is beyond the power of science to understand is far from straightforward.

One of the most impressive accomplishments of physics has been in devising a theory of gravity. This was the first theory involving one of the four forces that we currently know exist; the others being electromagnetism and the strong and weak nuclear forces. I know of no better way to introduce some of the ideas that will appear in this book than by referring to what I consider to be one of the most interesting, enjoyable, and thought-provoking stories it has ever been my pleasure to read.

Nightfall[1] is one of the classic stories of science fiction. It was written by Isaac Asimov while he was simultaneously working in his father's candy store and attending Columbia University. By this time, Asimov was so well-established as a writer of science fiction that he was asked by John Campbell, the editor of *Astounding Science Fiction*, to write a story.

Isaac Asimov might well be better known to the readers of this book as a popularizer of science, which constituted his primary output in his later years. His writings verge on encyclopedic; I think I read somewhere that philosophy was the only major subdivision of the Dewey Decimal System in which one could not find a book he had written. Although Asimov was not the first popularizer of science—I think that honor goes to Paul de Kruif, who wrote the classic book *The Microbe Hunters*[2]—he was almost certainly the first one to achieve widespread acceptance. I was tremendously flattered when one reviewer compared my book *Cosmic Numbers* favorably with some of Asimov's writings.

At any rate, being asked by an editor to contribute anything is a sign that you've arrived as a writer, even if you are still working in your father's candy store. Campbell had been thinking about a quotation attributed to Ralph Waldo Emerson: "If the stars should appear one night in a thousand years, how would men believe and adore, and preserve for many generations the remembrance of the city of God which had been shown!"[3] Campbell disagreed with Emerson, feeling that men would instead go mad. He discussed this with Asimov, who then penned *Nightfall*.

The story was written in 1941. I have given a reference to it in the Notes on page 239, and because it is such a terrific story and stands up so well, I won't spoil it for you by relating the plot. However, there is a key aspect to the plot which is germane to this book. The setting for *Nightfall* is Lagash, a planet which weaves a complicated orbital path in a system which is lit by six stars. The astronomers and physicists of the planet have, after 400 years of work, managed to deduce the Theory of Universal Gravitation. Interestingly enough, science fact followed science fiction last year.

The planet Kepler 16b is now known to orbit two stars,[4] the first planet known to do so.

We, too, have deduced the Theory of Universal Gravitation. There were four main players involved in teasing out the first of the great laws of physics that scientists have formulated. The first participant was Nicolaus Copernicus, a Polish scientist who enunciated the heretical theory that the Earth was not the center of the Universe, and that the Earth and the other planets revolved about the Sun. His epic work was published in 1543. Curiously enough, Copernicus died on the very date that he was presented with an advance copy of his soon-to-be-published book.

The heliocentric theory, as Copernicus' proposal came to be known, was in direct conflict with the teachings of the Catholic Church, which held that the Earth was at the center of the Universe. As a result, public espousal of the theory met with disapproval from the Church, and during this era, the Church had unpleasant ways of disapproving. For instance, Giordano Bruno, a leading proponent of the heliocentric theory, was burned at the stake in 1600 for an idea directly relating to his belief. He took Copernicus' theory a dramatic step further, proposing that the Sun was only one of an infinite number of worlds, some circled by planets as is the Sun, and populated by intelligent beings. Removing Earth from its central place in the Universe and relegating it to the status of just another world was regarded as heresy. Nonetheless, the heliocentric theory gradually gathered support from the leading scientists of Europe.

The second major character was Tycho Brahe, a Danish nobleman with a keen interest in astronomy. Born three years after the death of Copernicus, Brahe constructed Uraniborg, an astronomical observatory which could well lay claim to being the first research institute (although there may have been one at the Library at Alexandria almost two millennia earlier). Brahe systematically collected data and actually constructed a paper-making factory so that he might have enough paper to record his observations. This data was to prove invaluable in constructing the Theory of Universal Gravitation.

Brahe's research assistant in his later years was Johannes Kepler, the next actor to cross our stage. Kepler spent 20 years culling through Brahe's data, organizing and reorganizing it. This was not an easy task, as it was complicated by Kepler's convoluted family life: among other things, he was forced to defend his mother, who was accused of being a witch. With typical thoroughness, Kepler refuted the charges and managed to obtain an acquittal. You might think that it was difficult to prove that someone was a witch, but Kepler wasn't operating in the American system of jurisprudence, in which the defendant was presumed innocent.

The results of Kepler's labors are known as Kepler's Laws of Planetary Motion. The First Law states that every planet travels in an ellipse around the Sun, with the Sun at one of the foci of the ellipse. If you point a flashlight directly at the floor or the wall, the illuminated area forms a circle. Tilt it a little so that the lighted area elongates, and the curve formed by the boundary of the light is an ellipse. If you have ever been to a whispering gallery in a museum, the walls of the gallery are in the shape of an ellipse, and the two platforms where the whisperers stand are the foci of the ellipse. Kepler's other two Laws are more mathematical in nature, and only Kepler's First Law is relevant to this story.

The lead actor in the Theory of Universal Gravitation is Sir Isaac Newton, arguably the greatest scientist in history. Newton certainly doesn't need me to champion his claim, so I'll let Michael Hart, author of the wonderful book *The 100*, do so.[5] Hart compiled a list of the most influential people in human history. Newton is ranked third on Hart's list, and the only two people ahead of him are the two most influential religious figures in human history: Mohammed and Jesus Christ.

Newton died roughly 300 years ago, but if all you knew about math and science was what Newton had contributed, you'd be much better educated in both of these subjects than most inhabitants of this planet. What Newton did was absolutely extraordinary. He was able to provide a single, succinct description of how gravity acts, and from this description was able to deduce Kepler's Laws. The Theory of Universal Gravitation is one of the great intellectual achievements of the human race, requiring nearly 125 years from the time Copernicus first propounded the heliocentric theory until the theory was completed by Isaac Newton. Yes, Einstein did modify Newton's Theory of Universal Gravitation when he constructed his Theory of Relativity, but Newton's theory does an excellent job of describing all but the most extreme phenomena. We went to the Moon and sent rockets on complicated voyages to the planets (and beyond!) using Newton's theory.

Copernicus was a revolutionary, Brahe was a painstaking gatherer of data, Kepler was skilled at seeing underlying patterns in the data, and Newton was incomparably brilliant. Yet the four of them had an undeniable advantage over the scientists in *Nightfall*, for we live in a planetary system with a single Sun. One can imagine the difficulties of the task confronting the scientists in *Nightfall*. Their planet, Lagash, traces a tangled orbit among six suns. The Earth travels in an ellipse, with the Sun at one of the foci. An ellipse is a relatively simple curve to describe, as the example of the flashlight shows. It is also relatively simple to describe mathematically when one does so using analytic geometry. Despite this simplicity, it required many years before Kepler could divorce himself from the hypothesis that the planets traveled in circles about the Sun. Circles, after all, are among the simplest geometric figures, and the most straightforward heliocentric theory had the Earth and the other planets moving in circular orbits about the Sun. Kepler tried for years to fit circular orbits to Brahe's data, with poor results. After years of frustration, he changed his tack and decided to use ellipses rather than circles. In so doing, he set the precedent for one of the fundamental operating principles of science: trust the data, not the theory. It's a lot easier to do now than it was early in the 17th century.

It is hard to imagine how difficult the task of deducing the simplicity of the Law of Universal Gravitation would be, given the data that confronted the scientists of *Nightfall.* I would imagine that it would require major computer power today to describe the path of a planet under the influence of six Suns. In fact, there is a well-known problem of considerable mathematical difficulty known as the three-body problem, in which one tries to predict the orbits of three planets (or stars) in a Universe where these are the only three objects!

Even if one were sufficiently brilliant to come up with the correct hypothesis concerning the gravitational force, it would still have required an incredible amount of work to substantiate that hypothesis. One would have to know the masses of the six suns and the *Nightfall* planet, and have sufficiently accurate data, and computational ability, to deduce that planet's path. The *Nightfall* scientists mention that the task took 400 years—but the years on the *Nightfall* planet may be considerably longer than a year on Earth. A year on the planet Neptune, for example, lasts about 165 Earth years.

Deducing the Theory of Universal Gravitation on the *Nightfall* planet is indeed a difficult task—difficult, but not impossible. There would be a point, however, at which it would be impossible to deduce the Theory of Universal Gravitation, because there is a phenomenon known as the Butterfly Effect[6] which renders it impossible to perform certain computations exactly.

The equations that govern the behavior of the weather are much more complicated than the equations that govern gravitational attraction. They are also very delicately balanced; slightly different conditions at the start can create vastly different results sometime later. The Butterfly Effect is named after a description of the phenomenon given by Edward Lorenz, its discoverer, who gave a talk on whether a butterfly flaps its wings in Brazil might determine whether or not there is a tornado in Texas several weeks later.

It was later discovered that the Butterfly Effect is pervasive and applies to gravitational phenomena as well. We mentioned earlier that it is impossible to predict on which side of the Sun Pluto will be thousands of years from now[7]—and our solar system is relatively simple, considering that we only have one Sun and the masses of the planets are small in comparison. One can imagine a system with so many stars that it is simply impossible to predict where a planet will be some time later, and without the ability to confirm predictions it would be impossible to substantiate a Theory of Universal Gravitation. That does not mean that scientists living in such a system might not come up with the Theory of Universal Gravitation—after all, they might make a lucky guess. But they'd never know, and to them gravitation might seem to be a supernatural phenomenon.

Think about it: one of the reasons that we were able to deduce the Theory of Universal Gravitation is that the Earth follows essentially the same path around the Sun, year after year after year. This doesn't happen on the *Nightfall* planet, but the planet does follow an orbit sufficiently regular that its scientists were able to deduce the Theory of Universal Gravitation. The scientists on our hypothetical planet, the one with so many stars that the orbit is basically unpredictable, would in all likelihood never be able to work out the underlying simple law that is the Theory of Universal Gravitation. Even if they could, they could never confirm it.

But now we come to the crux of the matter. Just because gravitation appears to be a supernatural phenomenon to scientists living in an environment where the Butterfly Effect would make it impossible to predict how gravity behaves, does not mean that gravitation is a supernatural phenomenon. In fact, we here on Earth know it isn't (as do the scientists on the *Nightfall* planet). And therein lies the problem for us, and it is a problem which investigators of the supernatural have recognized for some time. Just because we cannot explain a phenomenon, or even if we can never explain the phenomenon, does not mean we are dealing with the supernatural. There may well be an underlying simple—and perfectly natural—explanation for the phenomenon, consistent with natural laws that we have not yet discovered, or, in fact, may never discover. One can imagine debates on our imagined planet, the one with so many stars that it is impossible to predict where celestial objects will be. Philosophers, scientists, and religious figures could argue whether sunrises, sunsets, and eclipses are natural or supernatural phenomena.

The scientists on our imaginary planet may indeed be able to make an educated guess about the Law of Universal Gravitation. Coulomb's Law, which is the law that relates the electric force between two electrically charged objects, turns out to have exactly the same mathematical form as Newton's Law of Universal Gravitation. The only difference between the two formulas is that Newton's Law uses the letters m_1 and m_2 to denote the two masses; Coulomb's Law instead has the letters q_1 and q_2 to denote the two electrical charges. Other than that, the two Laws have exactly the same formula! In fact, it is probable that Coulomb knew the form for Newton's Law and used that form to hypothesize the law governing electric charge. It would not be a wild leap for a scientist on our imaginary planet, assuming that they have discovered Coulomb's Law, to conjecture that the Law of Gravitation has a similar form.

Nonetheless, they may not get around to this approach, and unless they are able to travel to a system where gravitation is a simple phenomenon, they may erroneously classify gravitation as supernatural. How can we be sure that we are not making the same mistake for different types of phenomena?

So we now have a natural law, the Theory of Universal Gravitation, which was discovered with much effort on Earth (even more effort on the *Nightfall* planet) but which is essentially undiscoverable on the planet where the Butterfly Effect renders it undiscoverable. But even though there are (hypothetical) planets where it would be impossible to discover the Theory of Universal Gravitation, that Theory nevertheless exists. There's a slight linguistic problem here concerning whether the Theory is the way gravity actually is or the way that we describe how gravity actually is. There is gravity, there is Newton's Theory of Universal Gravitation, and there is Einstein's Theory of Relativity. We are obviously producing ever more accurate descriptions of gravity, but can we be certain that at the moment we have a description of gravity that tells us exactly how it is?

Possibly there is an ultimate Theory of Universal Gravitation to which Newton's Law was an excellent first approximation and Einstein's Theory of Relativity a distinctly superior modification, but we still haven't found it. Nonetheless, both Newton's and Einstein's theories are classified as scientific laws. A scientific law doesn't have to be a perfect description, but it has to work extremely well and extremely often.

Here, however, is the $64,000 question—at least as it pertains to this book. Is there a natural law out there which cannot be discovered? There is a point to phrasing the previous sentence in the passive voice. Had I said, "Is there a natural law which we cannot discover?" there might be the inference that we're just not bright enough to plumb the ultimate secrets of the Universe. But a law which is a law but which cannot be discovered would legitimately be supernatural. It would be a principle governing behavior in the Universe which would be beyond our ability, or the ability of any sentient creature, to discover.

And that's what I claim in this book. There are hypotheses about the physical Universe which I claim result in laws—governing principles—which cannot be discovered, by us or by any sentient creature. If you look at the strict dictionary meaning of "super" as it comes from the Latin, it means "above" or "beyond." I would argue that governing principles in the Universe that lie beyond the ability of science—any science—to discover are supernatural. In the literal sense, it fits the definition of supernatural, far more so than alien abductions or strange doings in the Bermuda Triangle. I can't see why it wouldn't fit your definition of "supernatural" as well.

5 The Search for Patterns

The search for underlying order goes back beyond recorded history. Underlying order—its discovery, explanation, and hopefully its use in productive enterprises—is the goal of science. Underlying order is often manifested in patterns. And that's where mathematics enters the picture.

In 1988, *Science* magazine, the official publication of the American Association for the Advancement of Science, published an article by Professor Lynn Steen of St. Olaf's College. This article, entitled *The Science of Patterns*,[1] discusses the increasing role that mathematics plays in the sciences. This role has continued to expand in the 25 years since this article was published.

The patterns that mathematics discovers are relationships between mathematical objects. As they are the result of mathematical reasoning, if the reasoning is correct and the assumptions on which they are based lead to no contradictions, the patterns themselves must be correct. There have been hundreds of different proofs of the Pythagorean

Theorem, that in a right triangle the square of the hypotenuse is the sum of the squares of the other two sides. This pattern is true for every right triangle and indeed, it characterizes right triangles. If you stumble upon a triangle such that the square of one side is equal to the sum of the squares of the other two sides, you may rest assured that you are looking at a right triangle.

What about that business about the assumptions on which they are based not leading to any contradictions? That's an extremely important point; if you are working with a system of assumptions that is flawed in the sense that valid reasoning from them leads to contradictions, you have to discard that system of assumptions. The formal investigation of which systems of assumptions do not lead to contradictions is part of mathematical logic. We shall look at this more deeply in subsequent chapters, because part of the claim I am making is based on discoveries made in mathematical logic.

If there is a formula in the sciences that has the recognizability of the Pythagorean Theorem, it would certainly be Einstein's formula $E = mc^2$. Formulas are not icons with symbols; they have meaning. Many people recognize that formula and could tell you that Einstein had something to do with it, but could not tell you what it means, though what it means is critical to today's world. It's about the relationship between matter and energy. If you could convert 1 gram of matter completely to energy, Einstein's formula would tell you that you could produce about 9×10^{20} ergs of energy. For purpose of simplicity, we have rounded off the speed of light to 300,000 kilometers per second; it's actually a teeny bit less than that, but let's use that figure to illustrate the idea. 9×10^{20} is 9 with 20 zeroes after it; in realistic terms, the complete conversion of 1 gram of matter to energy would supply the lighting needs for a small town for about a year.

Are There Conspiracies in Nature?

A conspiracy, according to the dictionary, is a secret plan to do something dangerous or harmful. A conspiracy theorist tries to fit events into an underlying pattern. The more grandiose and all encompassing the pattern, the better. Many conspiracy theorists pinpoint one sinister organization as being responsible for many of the problems that beset the world.

Surprisingly enough, there is an analogue to such conspiracies in physics, although maybe "conspiracy" is not the appropriate word. Many physicists spend their lives in a quest for the Theory of Everything, a simple theory that would unify the major physical theories that describe the Universe. Such a theory would have to unify two of the most impressive theories that physicists have discovered. Relativity, Einstein's theory describing the workings of gravity, is the most successful theory to date of gravity. Profound and beautiful, it describes the world of the large, from the pull of the tides and the orbits of planets to the distortion of space and time around a black hole. Quantum theory describes the world of the small, the atom and the electron. Equally profound and beautiful, it is the most accurate theory of the Universe ever developed, describing some phenomena to an accuracy of nineteen decimal places. This is equivalent to knowing to the nearest penny how much is in a vault containing hundreds of quadrillions of dollars.

To date, these two theories have proved incompatible. No one has yet demonstrated how to merge the two of them, and this is an all-consuming quest for a segment of the physics community. Part of the problem is that gravity is an unbelievably weak force when compared to electromagnetism and the weak and strong nuclear forces that govern the behavior of subatomic particles. Yes, if you put two electrons (which have negative electric charges) near each other, their masses will cause a mutual gravitational attraction, which will be utterly overwhelmed by the electrostatic repulsion that occurs when two objects have similar charges. The electrostatic repulsion is roughly 39 orders of magnitude—1 with 39 zeroes after it—stronger than the gravitational attraction.

Many physicists admit that we still have a ways to go, but believe that we can achieve the goal of discovering a Theory of Everything. Both quantum mechanics and gravity apply to all objects in the Universe, and it's distasteful to apply one theory to heavy objects and one theory to lightweight objects. It's not as bad as applying one theory on weekdays and one theory on weekends, but it leaves a bad taste in the mouths of many physicists.

However, not everyone believes that there is such a Theory of Everything. The famous physicist Richard Feynman replied, "If it turns out there is a simple ultimate law that explains everything, so be it.... If it turns out it's like an onion with millions of layers, and we're sick and tired of looking at layers, then that's the way it is."[2]

Physicists who believe in, and search for, the Theory of Everything, are respected members of the community. It says something about the complexity of human affairs, when compared with the relative simplicity of the physical Universe, that scientists who look for a Theory of Everything are regarded as pursuing a fascinating and worthwhile goal, whereas individuals who look for the same type of theory concerning human events—which is exactly the object of the search for many conspiracy theorists—are generally regarded as somewhere between deluded and genuinely unbalanced.

For the moment, let's assume there is a Theory of Everything. Can this theory be discovered? If so, the Theory of Everything would undoubtedly be one of the most impressive achievements of the human intellect, now or ever. But what if this Theory of Everything could *not* be discovered? It would be a conspiracy of the highest order, an underlying pattern to events that would be forever out of our reach. We're back where we were in the previous chapter, when we wondered if there were relationships between physical parameters which could remain forever hidden. Could we ever know that there was such a Theory of Everything, without knowing what that Theory of Everything actually said?

How deep would such a conspiracy of Nature be? What can we infer from the fact that we've learned something—quite a lot, actually—about the workings of Nature? Going back to the problem we looked at in the last chapter, is there an ultimate natural law of gravity? After all, even if Relativity isn't the last word in gravity, it's pretty close. I daresay most physicists would bet there is such an ultimate law of gravity, whether or not they think that we need a theory of quantum gravity to adequately express it. Most physicists would also bet that we can discover it—maybe not tomorrow, or next year, but eventually. If we can discover the workings of one law and indeed there is an ultimate pattern, shouldn't we be able to discover it?

How We Confirm the Existence of Patterns

Let's get back to the result predicted by the equation $E = mc^2$, that the complete conversion of 1 gram of mass to energy results in 9×10^{20} ergs of energy. If you were able to perform a number of experiments in which you converted exactly 1 gram of mass completely to energy, it's extremely unlikely that you would obtain 9×10^{20} ergs every time you did this experiment. Due to the fact that no experiment is perfect and our measuring instruments have a certain amount of imprecision, you'd likely get a bunch of different numbers. Maybe one might be as low as 8.97×10^{20} ergs, another might be as high as 9.03×10^{20} ergs. But this is such an important formula that you'd like to be able to use it with reasonable assurance.

That reasonable assurance is supplied by statistics. There are several different ways to use statistics to supply you with that assurance, but most of them center around the idea of hypothesis testing. You can never be certain that $E = mc^2$, but you can perform enough experiments to deduce using statistical methods that the hypothesis that E is not equal to mc^2 is extremely unlikely. The hypothesis that E is not equal to mc^2 goes by the fancy name of the null hypothesis in statistics; when you establish that it is extremely unlikely, you are said to reject the null hypothesis. Rejecting the null hypothesis that E is not equal to mc^2 is not the same as actually verifying that $E = mc^2$, but given the constraints of reality it's the best we can do.

However, there still remains a question: how unlikely does something need to be before you can reject it? The answer to that question is generally the result of either an explicit or unspoken agreement by leading experts in the field. For instance, particle physicists are currently searching for evidence of an as-yet-unseen particle which gives mass to objects. Called the Higgs particle, they will only claim that they have evidence for its existence if existence-confirming results would happen by chance about one time in four million.

Things are different in the social sciences. Because of the difficulty of controlling the factors involved, the null hypothesis is rejected if positive results would only have occurred by chance one time in twenty. This means that it is far easier for an idea to become an accepted part of a social science, such as psychology, than it is for it to become part of a physical science.

If you are a critic of social sciences, the fact that the bar a theory needs to cross is lower for theories in social science than for theories in physical science gives you a certain amount of ammunition. On the other hand, because we haven't reached the point—and may never reach the point—where ideas in the social sciences can be verified to the same level of accuracy as in the physical sciences, without lowering the bar we'd have no worthwhile theories at all! Besides, if we regard the physical sciences as starting with the experiments of Galileo, the standard of accuracy for physical sciences then was probably lower than what the standard of accuracy for social sciences is now. Galileo used his pulse to measure time intervals when performing his famous experiments of rolling balls down an inclined plane; it's also unlikely that tools existed to measure distances to an accuracy much less than a quarter of an inch.

How Accurate Are the Predictions of Astrology and Numerology?

Numerology and astrology have something in common with quantum mechanics and relativity. These four subjects also have something in common with psychology and economics. They all represent an aspect of one of the oldest and most basic of human intellectual endeavor: the search for order in the Universe. As we've observed, order in the Universe makes itself known through patterns.

We can use statistics to test the accuracy of any prediction-making discipline, such as astrology or numerology. There have been a number of statistical tests made on astrology, rejecting a null hypothesis at the same level as one would in the social sciences. The people who made these tests acknowledged that they had some difficulty, because the practitioners of astrology do not agree universally on what astrology says. My favorite study on this subject is the paper *An Empirical Test of Popular Astrology*,[3] by Ralph Bastedo. His statistical tool of choice is the chi-square test for goodness of fit, which measures the degree to which the behavior of two variables are related. A typical example of what is tested in this paper is the hypothesis that those who are born under the zodiac signs of Leo, Aries, Scorpio, Capricorn and Sagittarius have leadership ability. Aries did extremely well with regard to leadership, but the other four were below average. The net result was that this prediction of astrology failed to be confirmed by statistical tests, as did other similar astrological predictions. I particularly enjoyed Bastedo's closing remarks:

> My dispassionate approach has been broad-minded, detached, unprejudiced, and unbiased. The methods I have used have been logical, rational, and trust-inspiring. I have incorporated my natural intelligence, genius, brilliance, and inventiveness in this truth-thirsting endeavor. Above all else, I have remained sincere, honest, idealistic, and serious in my never-ending quest for the truth.
>
> It could not be otherwise. Because I am an Aquarian. And Aquarians are like that.[4]

Who says statisticians have no sense of humor?

I am not aware of similar tests that have been made with respect to the predictions of numerology, but I suspect that if they were, the results would be the same, because numerology has roughly the same basis in fact that astrology does, and dates from roughly the same period. In fact, astrology is founded to a large extent on the ideas of the Greek philosopher and scientist Ptolemy, whereas many of the ideas of numerology reflect the philosophy of Pythagoras, which was expressed as "All is number." Pythagoras lived centuries before Ptolemy, so astrology is actually a more modern approach than numerology.

Culture Shock

In 1959, the British scientist C.P. Snow gave a lecture entitled *The Two Cultures*, which put forth the viewpoint that those interested in the humanities and the liberal arts generally gave short shrift to the discoveries of science. Snow's thesis probably had some foundation; most educated people have some familiarity with Shakespeare and Mozart, while generally only those who have specialized in a technical subject are familiar with the Second Law of Thermodynamics or Newton's Laws of Motion. Most, possibly all, of those who believe in astrology or numerology come from outside the ranks of science and engineering; it's practically Orwellian double-think to understand the basis for the Second Law of Thermodynamics and at the same time believe that 9 is the master number. Not impossible, but really, really, really difficult.

Yet someone who believes in astrology or numerology is, like the scientist, searching for order in the Universe and the patterns that manifest this order. Two big differences between them are how much education is needed to understand the patterns, and how much of a conflict between the actual way things are and what the patterns predict the person will tolerate before rejecting a potential pattern.

It doesn't require a great deal of education to practice astrology or numerology. As far as I can tell, the only skills required are a small amount of arithmetic and the ability to sort things into groups according to certain characteristics. I visited a few sites on how to cast a horoscope; it has some basic calculations to be done using a variety of tables. It's similar in form to the calculations you need to do in order to set your telescope to look at a particular astronomical object in the night sky: you work from a basic number and make arithmetic adjustments to that basic number based on specific conditions. The difference is that if you do it right, you get to look at the rings of Saturn in your telescope, whereas if you cast your horoscope correctly, the results it predicts are no better than chance.

If the results that a horoscope predicts are no better than chance, why bother? Well, if you are a believer, you will tolerate those errors—and the only possible antidote to belief that I know of is understanding. Even understanding doesn't always work. After all, a stopped clock is right twice a day, and if you look at your horoscope often enough, it will be right a certain percentage of the time. It will even be right a certain percentage of the time when it was really important that it be right—and those are the times that a believer will remember.

We Need More Keplers

One of the reasons that I am writing this book is in the hopes that it will be read by a modern Johannes Kepler. We've already met Kepler as one of the four individuals most responsible for devising the original theory of gravitation, but what wasn't mentioned previously was that Kepler was probably one of the foremost astrologers of his day (if, indeed, it is possible to make such a statement). As a student, he earned a reputation by casting horoscopes for his fellow students. Nonetheless, the Kepler who was intrigued by patterns as manifested through astrology morphed into the Kepler who discovered Kepler's Laws of Planetary Motion.

It is relatively easy to become a scientist these days, as science is a basic course in our public schools, and scientists are generally (but not universally) regarded as productive members of society. Consequently, an individual with the talent and inclination to become a scientist can generally manage to do so. But to become a scientist when your training and inclination point in another direction is much more difficult. Kepler had to overcome not only his initial focus on astrology, but his belief in certain theories that manifested patterns he felt to be of divine origin. For instance, Kepler knew from geometry that there were only five regular solids. A regular solid is an object all of whose sides are the same, and are either equilateral triangles, squares, or regular pentagons. Moreover, the sides must fit together so that the angles between any two sides is the same. The cube is the regular solid whose sides are squares, and the dodecahedron is a 12-sided object that looks a little like a soccer ball whose sides are regular pentagons. There are three regular solids whose sides are equilateral triangles: the four-sided tetrahedron (which looks like a pyramid), the eight-sided octahedron (which looks like an upward-pointing pyramid placed on top of a downward-pointing pyramid), and the twenty-sided icosahedron. There were also five planets known at that time other than the Earth: Mercury, Venus, Mars, Jupiter, and Saturn. Coincidence? Kepler thought not, and spent a tremendous amount of time trying to fit the orbits of the planets to patterns suggested by the regular solids.

It didn't work. So Kepler made the hard choice of trusting the ugly data rather than the beautiful theory. We are all beneficiaries of this decision, as it is unlikely that our technology would be as far advanced as it is without Newton having the benefit of Kepler's Laws with which to check his Theory of Universal Gravitation. Newton might well have developed his theory without having Kepler's Laws, but the general acceptance of that theory would not have come so quickly, and that's what kick-started our modern era.

Preaching to the Choir and Energizing the Base

I've written several books on science and mathematics, but they will have little effect on the world because they will not change anything. These books are mostly read by people already interested in science and mathematics, and you don't really accomplish anything significant by preaching to the choir. In advancing learning, it isn't necessary to perform the equivalent of what is known in politics as "energizing the base." "The base" refers to the core of people who fundamentally agree with you, no matter whether you are a conservative or a liberal. However, "the base" is often lethargic when it comes to actually voting, because voting requires effort. Therefore, it is necessary to make sure that "the base" actually votes, and this is done in one of two ways. Either one can convince "the base" how wonderful their candidate is and how important it is to support him or her, or—and this is more common—the opposition candidate can be demonized and "the base" convinced how important it is to defeat him or her.

As I've mentioned, it isn't necessary to energize the base in math or science. People who love these subjects and are capable of making contributions are going to do it, and they'll do it because it's what they love to do, not because it's necessary to frighten them by telling them how terrible the world will be should ignorance and superstition triumph. But, just as in politics, it's better to create a potential ally from someone who is not inclined to be a member of the choir. However, there's a problem here: how do you get someone who is not a member of the choir to even listen to you? One way—and let me make it very clear that this is *not* the way that I have selected—is to threaten them with punishment, while promising undreamed-of rewards, until you have convinced them to adopt your viewpoint. This worked for a lot of missionaries, but it won't work here. There is no possible threat that I can bring to bear on someone who has a greater appreciation of astrology than they do of astronomy. Among other things, astrology gives the individual guidance, and many people find satisfaction in that. Astronomy does nothing of the sort. Both astrology and astronomy study the Moon, but according to astrology, the Moon and its place in the Universe can supply guidance. According to astronomy, the Moon simply controls when the tide comes in and when it goes out.

However, there is one important difference that I have noticed between people to whom astrology plays a significant role and those who prefer to think about astronomy. It's the role that mystery plays. To someone of a scientific bent, a mystery is a puzzle awaiting solution. Then, it's on to the unraveling of the next mystery. People who are interested in astrology tend to appreciate mystery more—it's okay if there are unsolved puzzles—in fact, it even adds to astrology's allure. In the song *Aquarius* from the musical *Hair,* the lyric begins, "When the Moon is in the Seventh House, and Jupiter aligns with Mars, then peace will guide the planets, and love will steer the stars."[5]

I haven't investigated astrology closely enough to know if this is a correct astrological interpretation, but let's assume for the purpose of continuing the discussion that it is. Just reading those words gives a good feeling about the times to come (it helps that the tune is also quite pleasant), and to some extent this can serve the function of a self-fulfilling prophecy. If enough people believe that peace will guide the planets, then peace is almost certainly more likely to guide this particular planet. In fact, this was a characteristic belief that prevailed during the 1960s, whether you believed in astrology or not.

So let's suppose that you believe that when the Moon is in the Seventh House and Jupiter aligns with Mars, peace will guide the planets. Do you ask where this knowledge comes from? If you believe in the world view offered by astrology, I assume that you think there are guiding astrological principles which underlie this prediction. Where do these principles come from? Did the people who devised astrology compile a huge database from which they extracted important results, in the same way that it was shown that there was a high correlation between smoking and lung cancer? Almost certainly not. They just didn't compile huge databases back in those days, and even if they had, the statistical techniques needed to tease out the correlation between the astronomical data and events here on Earth hadn't even been invented yet. So either there must be some general principles of astrology by which astrologers reached the conclusion that when the Moon is in the Seventh

House, etc., or astrology was constructed through the use of a few observations.

My guess is that if there are guiding general principles for astrology, very few of the practitioners of astrology know what those general principles are. They are reasonably well versed in what they need to do to accomplish one of the fundamental goals of astrology: the casting of horoscopes. This is a fairly cut-and-dried procedure, requiring a certain amount of arithmetic manipulation and consultation of tables, but it isn't rocket science. As for the much larger number of people who pay attention to their horoscope and are to some extent guided by it, they are perfectly content to assume that this knowledge came from somewhere, and to let that remain a mystery. I suspect that many people who pay attention to their horoscope appreciate both the general principles of guidance and the aura of mystery that surrounds where this comes from. The phrase "wisdom of the ancients" is often invoked here. There's both mystery and allure to the "wisdom of the ancients."

There's almost no mystery or similar allure to the wisdom of the contemporaries. Contrast the number of movies and TV shows which feature an Indiana Jones or a Lara Croft seeking a mystical relic with presumed awesome powers constructed by a past civilization, with the number of movies and TV shows featuring a Watson and Crick trying to decipher the mysteries of DNA or Marie Curie unraveling the puzzle of radioactivity. Granted, there are a lot of exogenous variables floating around when we try to make the comparison—one can cast a Harrison Ford or an Angelina Jolie in the role of a fictional Indiana Jones or Lara Croft, but it's a little difficult to see Brad Pitt as James Watson (or Frances Crick) or Megan Fox as Marie Curie. Nonetheless, there's relatively no mystery to science as it stands, because science is an attempt to remove as much mystery as possible. But even though science is a continuing attempt to remove the mystery, by no means does it remove the allure.

The explorations of science have opened up worlds seemingly beyond belief. Nowhere in any of the writings of the great thinkers who lived prior to the 17th century do you find direct references to the world that was uncovered when Anton von Leeuwenhoek first trained a primitive microscope on a drop of pond water. Although many people during the last few centuries have speculated that there were other worlds circling other stars, it isn't until the last two decades that we have actually established that they exist, and only in the last few years have we actually seen them and found ones similar to Earth. Just in the last couple of years we have found planets which have surface temperatures in the range that makes it possible for life to exist.[6]

Wisdom of the Ancients

Astrology and numerology are, to say the least, looked on askance by the scientific community. However, the scientific community doesn't regard religion in the same light. Science and religion have very different world views, but ever since western religion stopped seeing scientific discoveries as direct challenges to the Bible, there has existed a détente between the two that has improved with the passage of time. The Templeton Prize, established in 1972, is awarded to individuals who expand the vision of human purpose and ultimate reality, as is stated on its Website.[7] It has gone to individuals of all faiths, to scientists who won the Nobel Prize and most recently to the Dalai Lama. The Vatican has switched from a policy of burning heretics at the stake (as it did to Giordano Bruno, who dared to suggest that the Universe contained other worlds populated by intelligent beings) to sponsoring conferences on astrophysics.

I think the reason that science has reached a truce with religion, but not with astrology or numerology, is because the positions that religions take are generally not amenable to hypothesis testing or other scientific tools for evaluation of right and wrong. Science generally stays away from questions that do not deal with objective reality; you'll never see a scientific experiment conducted to see whether Monet was a better painter than Rembrandt. Where science takes issue with both astrology and numerology is that they both make testable predictions, and these testable predictions have been consistently found to be no better than chance.

I don't have quite this level of antipathy with regard to astrology and numerology, partially because I see them in a different light. I look at astrology and numerology as disciplines that primarily offer life guidance, rather than objective views of reality. Science is not in the business of providing life guidance; it's in the business of providing information about the nature of objective reality. If someone wants to get their life guidance from reading the horoscope or computing their lifepath number, it's really no business of mine—even if it's not something that I would do. As I've mentioned, my family was not religious, and so life guidance for me at an early age consisted of an assortment of injunctions, such as "Eat your vegetables." In fact, the first exposure I had to an actual unified philosophy of how to conduct one's life came when I went for a haircut at the age of about 7, and opened a Donald Duck comic book in which several of the major characters were making decisions according to flipism. Flipism consisted of flipping a coin when one had a decision to make; I don't remember how it worked out for the protagonists, but I do remember thinking that it had the twin virtues of simplicity and clarity.

I took a look at the horoscope in today's paper. As these things go, it was pretty generic, "Today is a good day to make new friends, etc." How can you get upset by that? As far as I know, scientists don't take umbrage with the fortune cookies offered at the end of a meal in a Chinese restaurant, and they say pretty much the same type of thing. As long as astrology and numerology stick to life guidance, I'm not going to have a problem with them—or anything else of that ilk. Sure, there's always the chance that the new friends you make may turn out to be poor choices for friends, but nobody will blame astrology for that.

The wisdom of the ancients is almost certainly going to prove harmful when it supplies counsel that contradicts proven knowledge. One classic example of this is a preference for faith healing as opposed to sound medical practice. Western society has generally agreed that when you reach a certain age, you're entitled to make these decisions for yourself. If you are 21, and your doctor has counseled a certain course of treatment but you prefer to consult a faith healer, it's on you. However, Western society frowns—and with justification—on you making this decision for someone who is not competent to make that decision on their own, such as a child or an adult whose care has been entrusted to you.

The Uncrossed Threshold

There is still a threshold of mystery that science has not yet crossed, and that is the threshold that separates the natural from the supernatural, the normal from the paranormal. However, there is a long history of people whom we would classify as scientists who have felt that there was something to be gained from a study of supernatural or paranormal phenomena. Certainly Johannes Kepler was such an individual. I have already mentioned Brian Josephson, whose scientific credits are truly impressive. There have been many other similarly-inclined scientific heavyweights (and middleweights and lightweights as well). As I said earlier, when a number of respected scientists believe that a subject is worthy of investigation, we should be unbiased enough to examine their views and be objective about the results of their investigations. Those views and investigations form the subject matter of the next chapter.

6 Scientists and the Supernatural

Despite the fact that science is generally uncomfortable with regard to supernatural and paranormal phenomena, if telepathy and remote viewing are shown to be genuine phenomena, there will be a flood of scientists eager to investigate. I've already mentioned that the standard of proof for something to become an accepted part of science is extraordinarily high. This has been the case ever since the scientists of the 17th century—Newton, Boyle, Hooke, Galileo, Huyghens, von Leeuwenhoek, and a host of others—first systematized the process of collecting data, theorizing, and experimenting. Scientists know this, and yet numerous scientists throughout history, as well as many present-day scientists, have expressed a belief in supernatural phenomena. By definition, supernatural phenomena are part of the real world, yet lie beyond the scope of science. Let's take a look at the history of the interplay between scientists and the supernatural. There's no better place to start than with the man primarily responsible for the important role that science now plays in bettering our lives.

Isaac Newton

During Newton's lifetime, and indeed for some time thereafter, the boundaries of what is science and what is not science were not as clearly defined as they are today, and as we've seen, even today they're slightly muddled. There aren't many alchemists these days, but there were a whole lot during the Middle Ages and late as the 17th century. Isaac Newton, arguably the greatest scientist of them all, devoted at least a decade to the study of alchemy. It might have been considerably more, for many of his laboratory notes were destroyed in a fire. The great economist John Maynard Keynes purchased many of Newton's writings on alchemy when they went on sale at auction. After reading them, he offered the view that "Newton was not the first of the Age of Reason; he was the last of the magicians."[1]

That's a viewpoint with which I strongly disagree. No matter what Newton said about alchemy—and Keynes has the advantage of me there, because he read Newton's writings on the subject and I haven't—Newton was operating under the immense handicap that none of the critical experiments in chemistry had been performed. These experiments would put chemistry on the same sound footing that physics had achieved; a sound footing which was largely due to Newton's efforts. If Newton devoted years to a fruitless quest of the Philosopher's Stone (whose touch would turn lead into gold) and the Elixir of Life, I am willing to bet the farm that he did so because he felt that the methods that had proved so successful in physics would prove equally so in alchemy.

Any "top 10" list of the greatest scientists of all time would certainly include Isaac Newton; indeed, any individual who placed him lower than third on such a list would probably be in serious danger of having his or her license to vote on such a list revoked. Probably, Newton's best-known discoveries are his Law of Universal Gravitation and his Three Laws of Motion. Either one would undoubtedly entitle Newton to serious consideration for the "top 10" list, but Newton is also responsible for several of the centerpieces of mathematics, chief among them being his discovery of calculus. His mathematical contributions were not limited to discovering calculus, and he is also responsible for the first rigorous treatment of the science of optics. Not content with merely observing and theorizing, he also was a hands-on scientist and is responsible for the Newtonian telescope, which is still in use today.

Newton was full of contradictions. He had a healthy opinion of himself, and when some of his ideas were challenged or had others claim prior discovery, he could fight like a tiger. Yet he was often reticent to share his ideas. His work on the Theory of Universal Gravitation might never have seen the light of day had the astronomer Edmond Halley (who is best known for Halley's Comet, next appearing in 2061) not paid him a visit to ask Newton a question that was troubling him. Halley inquired of Newton what would be the motion of a body subject to an inverse square law of attraction. Newton told Halley that he had calculated that it would be an ellipse as part of his earlier work on gravitation, which was exactly what Kepler had discovered. Halley was so impressed that he underwrote the publication costs of Newton's *Philosophiae Naturalis Principia Mathematica*,[2] the work in which Newton detailed the Theory of Universal Gravitation. It's hard to say where we would be as a society if this book had remained in Newton's desk, to be discovered only after he died. Or, heaven forbid, if it were lost to posterity. We're very lucky it was the notes on alchemy that burned up in the fire.

Even when Newton would publish his ideas, he would sometimes do so anonymously. The mathematician Johann Bernoulli posed a problem to the mathematical community at large. Newton submitted a solution anonymously, but the solution was so elegant that Bernoulli immediately recognized that it was the work of Newton, declaring that "we know the lion by the mark of his claw."[3] Just as a composer or an artist has a style by which many of his or her works can be recognized, the same can be said of the great mathematicians and scientists.

Newton the person was full of contradictions, but Newton the mathematician and scientist was not. With one significant exception, everything he turned his hand to produced ground-breaking results. Newton's only significant failure was his protracted study of alchemy, in which he was basically doomed from the start. The technology to produce significant results in chemistry was simply not present at the time, and alchemy was operating from hypotheses which could not have led to fruitful results.

Even in an era when communication between scientists was limited by the speed of the fastest available transportation, horseback, Newton's fame spread throughout Europe. At times, Newton could be quite modest. He once remarked that "If I have seen further than others, it is by standing on the shoulders of giants."[4] He was, of course, referring to Archimedes, Copernicus, Kepler, Galileo, and all the other great scientists that preceded him. Though these were undoubtedly giants, Newton is now recognized as towering above them.

Newton is also known for a remark that is relevant for this book. When regarding his accomplishments—and he certainly was aware of how incredibly significant they were—he said, "I seem only like a boy playing on the seashore, and diverting myself in now and then finding a smoother pebble or a prettier shell than ordinary, whilst the great ocean of truth lay all undiscovered before me."[5]

It is very likely that all the great scientists—whether they be biologists like Charles Darwin or physicists like Albert Einstein—feel similarly. As a species, we have only been seriously in the science business since the days of Newton, about 350 years. Our best estimate is that the Universe has existed for a little short of 14 billion years, and a lot has happened in those 14 billion years.

Part of what has happened is that there's a lot of Universe. We now estimate that there are hundreds of billions of galaxies, and a typical galaxy contains hundreds of billions of stars. During the past two decades, we have discovered hundreds of extra-solar planets, and we now believe that the Sun is not atypical in that it is the center of a planetary system. And there's some really interesting developments occurring on at least one of those planets—ours! Life has emerged, and considering what we have learned about the complexity of a single cell, there's a great undiscovered ocean of truth remaining in the miniscule volume occupied by even the simplest of the single cells.

We have every reason to be proud of what we have learned during the 350 years since Newton first began working on the Theory of Universal Gravitation. In the arena of physics, we believe we have a description of the matter and forces that comprise the Universe. We have discovered how natural selection guides the evolution of species, and have unraveled the mysteries of the genetic code. There was a time when some scientists believed that we were nearing the end of the road of discovery. Max Planck, as a young student, decided that he was interested in physics, and asked Philipp von Jolly, one of the leading physicists of his day, about the prospects for study in this field. Von Jolly told Planck that almost all the great discoveries had been made, and all that remained was to fill in a few minor holes. It is highly unlikely that any scientist today would make such a claim; we have learned that almost every question that is answered unlocks the door to a host of unanswered ones. Some of the truly great questions have almost certainly not yet even been asked.

Scientists look at things scientifically—at least, they look at most things scientifically, especially the things which are capable of being measured and for which constructive theories can be formulated. However, most of us are capable of holding opposing views which are not completely reconciled—as long as they are not out-and-out mutually contradictory—and scientists are no exception. There are many scientists today who are devoutly religious, just as there have been in the past. Although religion and science are not mutually contradictory, it does seem to require a suspension of the scientific viewpoint in order to believe some of the things that religion asks of its followers. Christianity tells its followers that Jesus turned water into wine and fed a multitude with only a minimal amount of food. Judaism asks its adherents to believe that even though there was only enough oil for one day's worth of light in the lamp, it actually burned for eight days. I have asked several scientists of differing faiths about this, and most simply compartmentalize the claims of religion, rendering unto science that which is science's, and unto religion that which is religion's. Although my sample is admittedly small and biased (in the sense that all the individuals involved are people I know), I suspect that this approach to religion is fairly common among those scientists who are religious.

There is certainly some overlap between religious belief and belief in the supernatural, and this overlap exists independently of the degree of conviction that one has in science. Although I do not consider myself qualified to talk about religion in any depth, I'm pretty sure that Christianity and Judaism are representative in that they require faith on the part of their believers to accept events that are not in accordance with everyday experience, and probably not in accordance with established principles of science. One day's worth of oil simply will not burn for eight days, and water cannot be transformed directly into wine through ordinary processes. The deities of both Christianity and Judaism are both omniscient and omnipotent, and generally some demonstration of superior knowledge or superior power is needed to convince people—and it's not clear that a demonstration of superior knowledge would be accepted as easily as a demonstration of superior power. Something demonstrably outside of ordinary experience is needed.

To the extent that religion incorporates events that contradict everyday experience and known scientific laws, it touches on the supernatural. However, it is certainly possible to believe in the supernatural without requiring any sort of religious belief. Supernatural phenomena transcend the ability of science to explain them, but do not require the existence of a deity.

Unpopular Viewpoints

This brings us back to the question of why some scientists, whose careers and often lives are tied up with the natural, are willing to not only believe in the supernatural, but are also willing to investigate it, often with the same objectivity that they bring to the investigation of the natural. This is also a good time to repeat something to which I alluded at the outset of the book: the supernatural is generally regarded by science as a whole with disfavor. Science is a human occupation pursued by human beings, and even though science as a whole is rational and objective, there are many instances in the history of both science and mathematics in which certain investigations have been viewed with disfavor because they contradict the existing paradigm.

There are two well-known examples from science in the 20th century that come to mind with regard to the social pressure that the scientific community sometimes brings upon those who hold positions contradictory to prevailing theories. One of these is Alfred Wegener's theory of the continental drift. Alfred Wegener was a respected meteorologist who had made a study of the shapes of continents, and came to the conclusion that the continents at one time were close together but over the eons had drifted apart. This theory was ridiculed at the time, but has now been shown to be correct. Of more significance to contemporary society was the development by Jonas Salk of a polio vaccine. Salk's polio vaccine used an inactivated virus, contradicting the generally held belief at that time that only a live virus could be used to produce an effective vaccine. To an outsider, this may not seem to be such a significant matter, but Salk became famous by going against the prevailing paradigm, and never received the recognition from his peers that he did from the outside world. He received no Nobel Prize and was never elected to the National Academy of Sciences, which is rather surprising in view of the fact that he created a vaccine for a disease which at its peak crippled 60,000 Americans, and killed 3,000, in a single year.

Mathematics may be purely rational, but its investigators have their personal axes to grind as well. One of the most innovative mathematicians of the 19th century, Georg Cantor, developed the first legitimate mathematical treatment of infinite quantities. His work was not highly regarded by his colleagues; indeed, he was relegated to the minor leagues of 19th century German academia and suffered mental health problems as a result. Today, his work is regarded as fundamental. I mention Cantor specifically because his ideas are relevant to the hypothesis put forward in this book.

Scientists pursuing ideas that are out of the mainstream of a particular discipline, such as did Wegener and Cantor, face an uphill battle to get their ideas accepted, but no one would accuse them of not doing legitimate scientific activity. Scientists who pursue investigations that are not felt to be part of science run the danger of not being taken seriously, and may find themselves professional outcasts. As a result, even though many scientists may believe in the existence of supernatural phenomena, they realize that if they pursue investigations along this line and attempt to promulgate them at conferences or in journals, they are liable to discredit themselves with the scientific community. Science is essentially a highly conservative activity (even though many scientists are very liberal), and departure from orthodoxy is frowned upon.

The Victorian Era

Although science as we know it began to be pursued in the 17th century, it wasn't really thought of as science but as "natural philosophy," and most of its practitioners were relatively well-to-do gentlemen. By the 19th century, though, science had become an accepted part of mainstream culture, as well as a driver of technology and industry. The Victorian Era is sometimes known as the Age of Science, when a prevailing belief was that the Universe was governed by an assortment of natural laws. This is not surprising, since this was the era in which electromagnetism was first thoroughly understood. The laboratory investigations of Faraday and Oersted had culminated in the distillation of the laws of electromagnetism by James Clerk Maxwell, and this became a template for how science should work in the discovery of natural laws. Experimentation would be followed by the synthesis of the experimental results into a coherent theory.

Yet the Victorian period was also one of intense interest in the supernatural. This resulted in two very different views of the supernatural. One school held that supernatural phenomena were beyond the capability of science to analyze, while the other felt that science was capable of analyzing these phenomena and producing a coherent theory to explain them. The novelist Edward Bulwer Lytton felt that spirit manifestations, such as seemingly occurred during séances, should be investigated in a scientific fashion. If the phenomena were genuine, they should be susceptible to analysis.

Robert Hare

In the course of writing this book, I wanted to find out which scientists had a belief in the paranormal and the supernatural, and to what extent they had investigated them. Most of the names were known to me, but I had never heard of Robert Hare. During the middle of the 19th century, most of the significant work in chemistry was being done in Europe, but Robert Hare was the closest thing America had to a big-league chemist. That was a period of significant interest in spiritualism, during which some eminent scientists became interested in psychic phenomena. In 1855, Hare published a book with the partial title *Experimental Investigation of the Spirit Manifestations, Demonstrating the Existence of Spirits.*[6] Hare described how he started his investigations as a nonreligious skeptic, but as a result of the investigations became a religious believer. Needless to say, his scientific colleagues were less than thrilled with regard to Hare's conversion to spiritualism, but were able to dismiss it on the grounds that Hare, who was getting on in years, had succumbed to the infirmities of age. Hare was in his early seventies when that book was written, and the vigor and mental acuity of people in their seventies was considerably lower, in general, than what it is now.

Alfred Russel Wallace

If you haven't heard of Alfred Russel Wallace, it's because although Wallace was an extremely distinguished naturalist, he was also an incredibly unlucky one. Wallace deserves to be recognized as the co-discoverer of evolution through natural selection, along with Charles Darwin. Wallace spent a number of years in Brazil and had amassed a large collection of specimens to bring to England to help support the idea of natural selection. Unfortunately, Wallace booked his passage back to England on a ship which caught fire on the way back, and Wallace's collection was destroyed. While back in England, Wallace communicated some of his ideas to Darwin, who recognized that the two of them had come to essentially the same conclusion. Wallace published a paper; Darwin published the book *The Origin of Species*[7]—and the rest is history. One of the things that I took from this episode is that you have a better chance of favorable publicity if you publish a book than a paper—unless, of course, you're Albert Einstein. Which I'm not.

Wallace had begun investigations into the world of psychic phenomena early in life, and his advocacy of spiritualism strained his relations with his scientific colleagues, much as Hare's book did with his. Like Hare, Wallace became a believer in spiritualism. Wallace's sister also "discovered" Agnes Nichol, a young woman who conducted séances in Wallace's home that Wallace considered to be conclusive evidence of paranormal phenomena. Wallace wrote of these in a letter to the English physicist John Tyndall, who was an expert in magnetism:

> During the last two years I have witnessed a great variety of phenomena, under such varied conditions that each objection as it arose was answered by other phenomena. The further I inquire, and the more I see, the more impossible becomes the theory of imposture or delusion. I know that the facts are real natural phenomena, just as certainly as I know any other curious facts in Nature.[8]

And just what were these "great variety of phenomena"? Just what you would expect to see if you went to any séance (then or now) or watched a CGI séance in a TV show dealing with psychic phenomena (and there are a bunch). Levitation, table tilting, strange noises—but according to Wallace, Nichol was also able to produce fresh flowers and fruits in the middle of winter, a task not as easy in the 19th century as it is now.

William Crookes

William Crookes was a highly respected chemist and physicist. As a chemist, he discovered the element thallium; there are very few individuals who can claim to have discovered a new element, considering only 92 occur naturally and many (such as iron, copper, silver, gold, and mercury) have been known for millennia. As a physicist, he devised several important pieces of equipment, most notably the Crookes tube for the study of cathode rays. He was also the editor of several prestigious journals.

In 1870, Crookes announced his intention to conduct a scientific investigation of spiritualism, the belief that the spirits of the dead can communicate with the living. This belief had many adherents, and also led to the profusion of con artists conducting séances and table-tapping sessions with the intent of separating the gullible from their assets—a practice which goes on to this day. Crookes held the view that other forces operated in the natural world—distinct from the forces of gravity and electromagnetism which had already been analyzed to great effect. As Crookes put it, "New forces must be found, or mankind must remain sadly ignorant of the mysteries of Nature. We are unacquainted with a sufficient number of forces to do the work of the Universe."[9] In a way, Crookes was right, the weak and strong nuclear forces were yet to be discovered and play a prominent role in doing the work of the Universe, most notably in nuclear and thermonuclear reactions. However, this was almost certainly not what he had in mind. Crookes' remark that new forces must be found to do the work of the Universe goes to the heart of what many feel is the rationale for the paranormal and the supernatural, and there will be occasions to refer to it throughout this book.

Nonetheless, Crookes, who was remarkably astute in scientific matters, was considerably less so when it came to the many séances he attended. He was especially impressed by those conducted by Florence Cook, a medium who would go to a curtained-off section of the séance room, where she could not be seen by those attending the séance. Some time thereafter, a woman wearing a white robe and turban would appear, who claimed to be the materialized spirit Katie King. When you read an account like this, it certainly causes you to wonder if King and Cook were the same person. Crookes claimed that he had actually seen King and Cook simultaneously, but even if he had not observed them together, there were significant differences between the two, and so they could not be the same individual. King was taller, had much lighter skin, and wore different jewelry. On reading Crookes' comments, it is difficult to believe that they are written by the same individual who paid such exquisite attention to detail in the laboratory.

The Society for Psychical Research

The Society for Psychical Research was founded in 1882 by a number of prominent British intellectuals who were interested in what we would describe as paranormal phenomena. The Society, which is still in existence and maintains a Website, considers its primary fields of investigation to be mental phenomena, such as ESP and telepathy, and what is nowadays referred to as ADC (after-death communication).

The list of its past presidents, who can be assumed to be amenable to the fields of investigation described above, is quite impressive. I did not recognize all of the individuals, but it included a Prime Minister of England (Arthur Balfour), several philosophers and religious leaders, and many eminent psychologists, including the Americans William James and Professor Joseph Banks Rhine of Duke University. Rhine conducted an extensive series of experiments pertaining to ESP which will be detailed in a later chapter.

There were also a number of distinguished scientists, including William Crookes. Probably the best known was John William Strutt (Lord Rayleigh), whose contributions to mathematics and physics were voluminous. Rayleigh was one of the early winners of the Nobel Prize; even though the bulk of his contributions were in the study of waves in various surfaces, he received the Nobel Prize for his discovery of the element argon. During the period of the founding of the Society, Rayleigh spent some time investigating both how people were influenced through hypnotic suggestion and the performances of various mediums. He came away from these with something similar to the viewpoint that I currently hold: although in general he found the results unconvincing, he admitted that there were incidents that he found difficult to explain.

Another president of the Society was the physicist Sir Oliver Lodge. Lodge had made significant contributions to the study of electromagnetism, including obtaining several patents related to wireless telegraphy. He was also an early advocate of the length contraction hypothesis, propounded by his friend George Fitzgerald, that was to play a significant role in the development of the theory of special relativity as formulated by Albert Einstein. Obviously a respected member of the scientific establishment, Lodge is also known for his attempts to investigate such phenomena as telepathy and life after death. His dual role of scientist and investigator of the supernatural was perplexing to many of his colleagues. George Foster, a fellow professor of physics, undoubtedly spoke for many of his colleagues when he asked Lodge, "Is not the whole progress of physics based on the assumption that [Spiritualistic] things do not happen?"[10] Lodge shared his interest in the afterlife with Sir Arthur Conan Doyle, the author of the Sherlock Holmes stories. Lodge and Doyle were connected by their interest in the afterlife, possibly because each had a son who died during World War I.

Despite the fact that the Society is still in existence, it is probably true that its heyday occurred from the time of its founding until perhaps half a century later. Nonetheless, interest in the phenomena that intrigued the Society has persisted to the current day, and there were some interesting forays into the world of the paranormal by scientists in the 20th century.

Albert Einstein

Albert Einstein, of course, is easily the best-known scientist of the 20th century. In fact, Einstein was selected by *Time* magazine as its Person of the Century for the 20th century. In a century marked by two World Wars and some of the most notable political figures of all time, that's pretty impressive.

For the vast majority of non-scientists, and probably for a number of scientists as well, Albert Einstein personifies science. The great discoveries of science unquestionably have a component of genius, and Einstein was the embodiment of what the public thinks of as a scientific genius. Einstein was perhaps fortunate to be born in an era when photography was widespread, and the generally disheveled look, the unkempt hair, the occasional smoking of a pipe, all helped to shape the public image of what a scientific genius should look like.

I remarked in the Introduction that Einstein wrote in a letter to the psychologist Jan Ehrenwald that physics could not *a priori* dismiss the existence of a phenomenon such as telepathy. Some years prior to this, Einstein had been asked by his friend Upton Sinclair to write an Introduction to Sinclair's book *Mental Radio*.[11]

Upton Sinclair was best known for his exposé *The Jungle*,[12] the book which won him the Pulitzer Prize, and almost as well known for being an outspoken advocate of Socialism; he was several times the Socialist candidate for President. Less well known was his interest in psychic phenomena. His wife, Mary Craig Kimbrough, believed she had telepathic abilities, and asked Sinclair to help her explore this phenomenon. Sinclair conducted three years of experiments and detailed the results in *Mental Radio*, in which he compared the phenomenon of telepathy to radio broadcasts, with one mind broadcasting and the other receiving.

Any sort of endorsement by Einstein for an idea was a pearl beyond price for the proponents of that idea. Einstein wrote a short preface to the German edition of *Mental Radio*, which was translated in the American edition as follows:

> The results of the telepathic experiments carefully and plainly set forth in this book stand surely far beyond those which a Nature investigator holds to be thinkable.... So if somehow the facts here set forth rest not upon telepathy, but upon some unconscious hypnotic influence from person to person, this also would be of high psychological interest.[13]

Einstein was quite probably familiar with the results that Rhine and other investigators had obtained, and the above passage is sometimes put forth as evidence that Einstein was a believer in ESP. I think that this represents sloppy interpretation. Einstein is not saying he believes in telepathy—in fact, he basically says the opposite in the sentence that begins "The results of the telepathic experiments...." However, he is saying that these results are interesting—not because they tell us something new about Nature, but because they possibly have a lot to tell us about people.

Harold Puthoff and Randall Targ

During the 1970s, there was heightened interest in paranormal investigations; it was part of the zeitgeist of the era. The Parapsychological Association, formed in 1957, became affiliated with the American Association for the Advancement of Science in 1969. The AAAS is as hard-headed a proponent of orthodox science as exists, and a good deal of opposition developed, especially in view of the fact that nothing resembling legitimate scientific discoveries ever came of parapsychology. Once again, the point needs to be made that nothing scientifically substantive has ever come of numerous objective and well-meaning investigations into the supernatural and the paranormal. However, the 1970s saw one extremely well-publicized investigation into the world of the paranormal, conducted by physicists Harold Puthoff and Randall Targ of the Stanford Research Institute. (It should be noted that although the two institutions are both located in Menlo Park, the SRI has no connection with Stanford University.)

Puthoff and Targ were respected scientists who had made significant contributions to the study of lasers; this was an era in which lasers were being developed, and did not do everything they do today, such as scanning items at the store to compute your bill. In 1974, they published the paper "Information Transfer Under Conditions of Sensory Shielding"[14] in the ultra-prestigious British journal *Nature*. Short of winning a significant prize, publication in *Nature* of an article is one of the most impressive things a scientist can do.

Among other things, this paper discussed experiments with the alleged Israeli psychic Uri Geller. Geller was one of the more enigmatic characters to surface in the 1970s. A young man with considerable personality, he appeared on many radio and TV broadcasts, demonstrating his supposed paranormal powers. One of his performances on the BBC was to be scrutinized by a team of scientists; for one member of the team, it was a life-changing experience.

John Taylor

One of the best books I have read on the subjects of science, supernatural, and the paranormal is *Science and the Supernatural*,[15] written by John Taylor. Taylor earned a PhD in physics at Cambridge and secured a position at King's College in London. He has done extensive research, recently specializing in neural networks, and has written numerous popular books on science.

The genesis of *Science and the Supernatural* was an appearance by Taylor on a BBC television show, during which Taylor's self-described function was to be a "scientific hatchet man" during a performance by the Israeli psychic and entertainer Uri Geller. During the program, Geller performed three show-stoppers. The first was his signature act, bending cutlery. A tray of assorted cutlery was brought onto the stage, Geller selected four solid forks, keeping one and giving the other three to the members of the panel (which also included the show's host and the eminent biologist, Lyall Watson). Geller suddenly claimed that Watson's fork was bending, and, as Taylor says, "I watched in utter astonishment as Geller gently stroked the neck of the fork to cause it to break into two pieces. I could have sworn that the fork had not been forcefully bent back and forth during the program and I am certain that the many viewers at their television sets would have supported me in this."[16]

Geller's next demonstration involved telepathy. He was handed a sealed envelope with a silhouette of a yacht inside, which he reproduced with perfect accuracy. Taylor states, "I was once more astonished by this prowess; it just could not happen."[17] Taylor begins the book by stating that belief in the supernatural is characterized by the two extremes of true believer and complete skeptic, and prior to the show he had counted himself unequivocally in the camp of the skeptic.

The last demonstration in the show involved broken watches. Geller clenched his fist and held them over the watches, willing them to start. Taylor was amazed as one of them did indeed start, and the second hand of another buckled under the watch crystal.

Taylor confessed that he did not see how the performance could have been a fraud and felt his world collapsing around him. Geller was performing feats that the orthodox science in which Taylor had believed his entire life said could not happen.

Although Taylor was at the time unaware of this, there are some simple explanations for what happened. After Taylor wrote *Science and the Supernatural*, another book *Paranormal Borderlands of Science*,[18] appeared, which contained explanations for all of the apparent miracles that Taylor had witnessed. One such explanation concerned the ability of Geller to start watches by will power alone. When I read of Geller's demonstration, I was every bit as amazed as Taylor was; yet the explanation is remarkably simple. The show took place in the 1970s, during an era when the vast majority of watches were mechanical. David Marks and Richard Kammann, in an article entitled *The Non-Psychic Powers of Uri Geller,*[19] made a survey of a number of jewelers. These jewelers reported that more than 50 percent of watches that are brought in to be repaired are not mechanically broken. In some of them, the cause of the watch stoppage is either gummed oil or badly distributed oil. One possible explanation is that Geller, an accomplished magician, handled the watches without being observed doing so. Jewelers have noticed that watches can frequently be restarted simply by holding them to warm them.

After the Geller performance, an even more startling (to Taylor) phenomenon occurred. The telephone lines to the BBC were swamped by people who claimed to either have witnessed similar phenomena or, like Geller, possessed the ability to duplicate what Geller had done. Taylor was stunned. How was it possible that attributes so unusual were apparently present in such a large number of individuals?

This show provided the impetus for Taylor to start a research project of his own: to examine the various supernatural and paranormal phenomena from the dispassionate standpoint of an objective scientist. Taylor abandoned his stated role of "scientific hit man" in an attempt to get to the bottom of supernatural and paranormal phenomena. If these phenomena were valid, Taylor would attempt to explain them; if not, Taylor would report that as well.

Maybe I'm looking at this with the benefit of hindsight (which, as someone once remarked, is notably more accurate than foresight), but there is something that occurred to me while reading the material I've summarized above. Geller, at this time, was a self-described psychic; the BBC show was cast as a demonstration of psychic phenomena. Geller currently classifies himself as an entertainer; if the BBC show were presented now, it would doubtless be labeled entertainment, much as magic shows are so labeled in Las Vegas. My wife and I visit Las Vegas frequently and have seen many magic shows, which I find tremendously enjoyable. I'm a confirmed skeptic, but one with no background in magic, and it's fun to try to figure out how they perform a particular trick. Sometimes I'm successful, most times not—but I have never spent a fraction of a second believing that these individuals have somehow figured out a way to bypass the laws of science in performing a particular trick. I don't believe Taylor would have, either, had the Geller performance initially been classified as entertainment.

Let me illustrate what I mean with my explanation of a trick I have seen done by several performers. The performer appears on stage with a very large and heavy object; let's say a 1957 Ford Thunderbird with very unusual décor to make it appear distinctive. Then there is a roll of drums, a build-up of music, a flash of light and a cloud of smoke—and the performer and the T-Bird have magically been transported to the balcony from the stage! Sometimes this trick is done in reverse, going from the balcony to the stage.

It requires a large amount of energy to move T-Bird and performer that considerable distance. That energy either comes from somewhere—in accordance with laws of physics—or (and this is my interpretation of the trick), it does not come at all! What would be much easier is simply to have a duplicate version of the T-Bird already installed on the upper balcony; after all, there's more than one 1957 T-Bird in existence. Either enough time is allowed for the performer to go from stage to balcony or, more likely, there's someone dressed up in the same outfit who looks enough like the performer to accomplish the deception. There are a tremendous number of Elvis imitators in Vegas, so there probably are a few people who look enough like the performer to make the trick appear believable, especially when the audience is looking at the imitator from a distance. None of us watch a magic show and think that the laws of science have been superseded. We know we've been fooled, but it's part of the show.

Taylor, however, saw the Geller performance under very different circumstances and during a very different era. The 1970s were a period of heightened belief in the supernatural and the paranormal. It was the dawning of the Age of Aquarius, and people were more open and less skeptical. At any rate, so impressed was Taylor initially that he wrote an early book, *Super Minds: A Scientist Looks at the Paranormal.*[20] *Science and the Supernatural* was written later, and represents a more orthodox investigative point of view. With that book, Taylor regained the good graces of the scientific establishment. The impression I get is that Taylor now regarded his short venture into the world of the paranormal in approximately the same way that you would if one of your embarrassing moments suddenly appeared on *YouTube* and went viral.

Where Are They Now?

As mentioned previously, Taylor has returned to the fold, having decided that his previous endorsement of paranormal abilities, as described in *Super Minds,* was in error. Russell Targ and Brian Josephson, however, have stayed the course. Targ has written a variety of books; according to his Website, his most recent book is *The Reality of ESP: A Physicist's Proof of Psychic Abilities.*[21] Josephson, whom we met in the Introduction, has been awarded a Nobel Prize, probably the highest accolade that the scientific community can bestow. He is head of the Mind-Matter Unification Project at Cambridge University and is on the Editorial Board of *NeuroQuantology: An Interdisciplinary Journal of Neuroscience and Quantum Mechanics.* During 2001, Josephson's views on the paranormal were aired in a booklet written in conjunction with the centenary of the Nobel Prizes (the first ones were awarded in 1901). Josephson wrote:

> Physicists attempt to reduce the complexity of nature to a single unifying theory, of which the most successful and universal, the quantum theory, has been associated with several Nobel prizes, for example those to Dirac and Heisenberg. Max Planck's original attempts a hundred years ago to explain the precise amount of energy radiated by hot bodies began a process of capturing in mathematical form a mysterious, elusive world containing 'spooky interactions at a distance,' real enough however to lead to inventions such as the laser and transistor. Quantum theory is now being fruitfully combined with theories of information and computation. These developments may lead to an explanation of processes still not understood within conventional science such as telepathy, an area where Britain is at the forefront of research.[22]

This did not sit well with mainstream physicists. David Deutsch, a respected expert in quantum mechanics at Oxford University, declared that Josephson's views were "...utter rubbish. Telepathy simply does not exist."[23] Josephson, however, believes that telepathy and other manifestations of parapsychology are real, and states that scientists are generally uncomfortable about certain ideas.

Having "made his bones" by winning a Nobel Prize, Josephson has no problem airing his unconventional views on these subjects. I have discussed these subjects off the record with a number of scientists, and there is certainly some support for the supernatural and paranormal, although most scientists realize that it is a career-threatening move to investigate such phenomena. Science expands through peer review, and although there is undoubtedly no set agenda for rejecting papers on these subjects, peer review is conducted under the hypothesis that the paper is guilty until proven innocent. Evidence for the paranormal and supernatural are generally weak—at least from the standpoint of the high level of proof required by science—and so most scientists, even if they believe in such phenomena, realize that they are probably "drawing dead" if they attempt to pursue such investigations.

It is interesting to contrast this with string theory, a hypothetical explanation of matter and forces that is the subject of intense investigation in physics. There are several different versions of string theory, but all share a common feature: instead of viewing the basic particles of Nature as 0-dimensional points, it regards them as 1-dimensional oscillating lines, like the vibrating strings on a guitar or a violin. Several years ago, I was fortunate to attend a lecture on string theory given at the California Institute of Technology by Edward Witten. Witten is one of the leading theoretical physicists in the world, and has the added cachet of having won a Fields Medal in mathematics. Fields Medals are considerably rarer than Nobel Prizes; they are awarded only every four years, and if the mathematical community doesn't feel that any work worthy of such an award has been done in the intervening four years, they don't award one.

The lecture I attended was presented as an introduction to string theory, and many of the attendees were Nobel Prize winners themselves (everybody wore one of the little badges with his or her name on it). The audience included not only physicists and mathematicians, but chemists, biologists, and other guests. At the end of the lecture, there was a question-and-answer session. Witten, who has spent almost as much time pursuing string theory as Newton did on alchemy, admitted that as yet there were no experimental results to demonstrate that the string theory model was an accurate depiction of the way things were. String theory struck some of the less mathematically-inclined members of the audience as somewhat strange, and one asked Witten if he believed that this was the way Nature really was. Witten replied that if he didn't think this was the case, he wouldn't have spent ten years investigating it.

Why are Witten and the other string theorists happily accepted into the mainstream scientific community, while Josephson and those who believe in the paranormal regarded in a substantially less favorable light? I believe it gets back to the matter of falsifiability. From the standpoint of the advance of science, there is absolutely nothing wrong with promulgating an erroneous theory. The history of science is littered with erroneous theories that have been proved wrong: humorism, geocentrism, the phlogiston theory, the luminferous ether, Continuous Creation—just to name a few. Nowadays, though, a theory must make testable predictions; it must give itself the chance of being proved wrong. String theory does that: it makes predictions about the Universe at both its smallest and largest scales. Critics argue that these predictions are incredibly difficult to substantiate or falsify—the technology needed to do so is considerably beyond our current reach—but at least string theory has been willing to expose itself to the slings and arrows of contradicting facts. If, as Crookes believed, that new (mental) forces must be found to explain the work of the Universe, someone has to come up with a theory involving those new forces that involves testable predictions. As of now, no such theory has emerged.

Nor have any verifiable examples of supernatural or paranormal phenomena emerged, and there is a long history of attempts to verify such examples. In 1922, the magazine *Scientific American* offered two $2,500 prizes. One of the prizes was for the first authentic photograph of a spirit made under test conditions, and the other for the first psychic to produce a "visible psychic manifestation." The second challenge was accepted by a psychic named George Valentine, who claimed that, in his presence, spirits would speak through a trumpet floating in a darkened room. Valentine was seated in a chair in a darkened room, but he was unaware that a switch had been rigged to signal if he left the chair. The signal was tripped, and Valentine did not receive the award.

The stakes have been increased. James Randi, a magician and a leading skeptic of paranormal phenomena, has offered a million dollars to anyone who can demonstrate that they have supernatural or paranormal abilities under appropriate test conditions. To date, no famous psychic has accepted the challenge.

While trickery or delusion are often promoted as explanations for paranormal phenomena, Richard Wiseman of the Committee for Skeptical Inquiry offers another possibility. Polls have shown that almost one person in six feels that they have had an encounter with a ghost, but only one person in a hundred reports seeing a genuine ghost (presumably of the sheet-wearing, chain-rattling variety, although perhaps others qualify). Most of the other encounters come under the heading of "tantalizing hints": wisps of smoke, shadows, creepy sensations. Wiseman argues that these are actually the byproduct of activity of our own brains. I'm certainly not an expert in this area, but I could even go beyond that—there is a great deal of the brain that is a holdover from previous stages of evolution when heightened sensory awareness played a much more important role in survival than it does now. Those people who believe they have had an encounter with a ghost could be experiencing these sensory sensations on a level below the threshold at which we actually understand the cause of those sensations. Many of us hear noises, and turn around only to notice that there is no apparent cause of the noise. In some instances there actually was no noise, but in others there was but we are unable to isolate the cause.

I am not in a position to say whether or not a testable theory of new mental forces will ever emerge, but I believe I can account for at least part of the reason that there are present-day scientists who are convinced of the reality of supernatural phenomena—and it also applies, to some extent, to scientists in the past who were likewise convinced.

Let's look again at Newton's quote, "I do not know what I may appear to the world, but to myself I seem to have been only like a boy playing on the sea-shore, and diverting myself in now and then finding a smoother pebble or a prettier shell than ordinary, whilst the great ocean of truth lay all undiscovered before me." Most scientists feel the same way; that what science has discovered—or will discover—is but an insignificant fraction of the truth that is available to be discovered. Fortunately, the "insignificant fraction" refers to the quantity of truth that we have discovered, but we have probably discovered a significant fraction of the truth that is important to our progress. I don't feel, as did Phillip von Jolly, that all that remains is to fill in a few insignificant holes in our understanding, but there is no question that discoveries such as the atomic theory, evolution, relativity, and electromagnetism are significant far out of proportion to the actual quantity of truth that they represent. Not all truths are equal in terms of their impact on our lives.

My guess is that scientists prior to the middle of the 20th century felt basically as did Newton; there was a great ocean of undiscovered truth that would probably never be revealed. In the 19th century, Auguste Comte made an attempt to delineate some things that would never be known. It was known at the time that the stars were immensely far away—distances which seemed even more immense in view of the fact that no man-made object other than a bullet (or other projectile) was capable of traveling at speeds more than a 100 miles per hour. As a result, Comte conjectured that the composition of the stars would never be known. Not long after, the German physicists Robert Bunsen and Gustav Kirchoff invented the science of spectroscopy, which enabled that composition to be revealed. This left the impression that hazarding a guess as to exactly what would never be known might be a risky undertaking, but it didn't change the fact that there was going to be a lot of undiscovered truth.

7 Conditions Under Which Supernatural Phenomena Must Exist

I must confess to a certain amount of trepidation in titling this chapter, as I have no wish to incur the opprobrium of the scientific community. They are—or have been—my colleagues for my entire professional career, and if this is a serious misstep on my part, I doubt that I can work my way back to acceptance, as did John Taylor.

On the other hand, this chapter is titled "Conditions Under Which Supernatural Phenomena Must Exist," not "Why Supernatural Phenomena Must Exist." There's a difference—the phrase "conditions under which" obviously refers to a set of circumstances which may or may not be true. I am convinced that supernatural phenomena must exist *under the hypothesis that the Universe is infinite*. This chapter is devoted to an explanation as to why I am convinced of that.

I've stated previously that I think there are two basic classes of people who will read this book: scientists and those without much of a background in science. I've also stated that at some stage I have to present enough of a technical explanation to give those of a scientific bent something to analyze. It's not a scientific theory if it's not falsifiable, and so I'm not completely sure that this qualifies as a scientific theory. In some respects, it's a little like string theory, whose falsifiable predictions are beyond the reach of current technology, but at least string theory makes falsifiable predictions.

Let's assume, for the moment, that the argument that I am going to present is logically a convincing one. At this stage, one possible counter-argument might be, "Even though there are no holes in the argument, it is not a scientific theory. It depends upon the assumption that the Universe is infinite, and currently we have no way to falsify that." I have a couple of different ways to rebut that.

First, I could claim that I realize that this is not a scientific theory, and that I never stated that I was presenting one. What I did was state that under hypotheses that many scientists would accept, supernatural phenomena must exist. The hypothesis that the Universe is infinite is accepted by many scientists; I will give specific examples later.

Second, as my argument develops, the reader will see that there may not be ways to falsify it, but there may be a way to prove it! That's because the argument depends not only on the assumption that the Universe is infinite, but also on certain results in mathematical logic.

Irving the Explainer

I first encountered the term *Irving the Explainer* in an episode of *The Rockford Files*, an extremely enjoyable 1970s TV series that starred James Garner as a somewhat down-at-heels private investigator. In one episode, appropriately titled *Irving the Explainer*, the plot became so involved within the first half-hour that not only the characters in the show but the viewers as well couldn't keep track of what was happening. This was deliberate on the part of the show's writers, who had a character simplify the proceedings for the other characters and the viewers. The term "Irving the Explainer" is Hollywood jargon for a character whose function is to clear up confusion in these situations.

Most teachers have a little Irving the Explainer coursing through their veins; one of the reasons that people become teachers is because they take pleasure in understanding a certain subject and want others to share that pleasure. I have a lot of Irving the Explainer coursing through my veins, and I couldn't write this chapter by just stating the idea. We Irving the Explainers have to explain it.

However, one of the things that we Irving the Explainers have learned to live with is that not everybody wants things explained. For those who feel that they're willing to accept that in an infinite Universe supernatural phenomena must exist, you can skip to the next chapter, where the argument is summarized in the first paragraph—although there will be a few references that will not make much sense unless you've read this chapter.

Supernatural Phenomena in a Finite Universe

The Universe is finite if it is finite not only spatially but in time. That means that it had to have a beginning, and it has to have an end. Admittedly, we don't know whether or not the Universe is finite, but let's assume that it is. I think I can make a pretty good argument that if the Universe is finite, there are no supernatural phenomena, and any law that governs the behavior of the Universe can, at least in principle, be deduced.

Whether science is conducted by humans, aliens, or supercomputers, it's still essentially the same idea. Collect data, and construct a theory to explain the data. In the real world, we generally ask that a theory make predictions, and see whether or not those predictions are upheld. However, it's not really necessary, because something may be so simple that there are only relatively few cases—and if we have a theory which explains those cases, that's all there is to it.

Let's look at a really dull finite Universe: the Universe of all possible tic-tac-toe games. There are a lot of them, but if a scientist were able to examine a collection of tic-tac-toe games, he or she would notice the following facts:

1. The difference between the number of Xs and the number of Os is at most 1.
2. The only games in which not all nine squares are filled either have three Xs in a row or three Os in a row.

Working on only this information, one possible explanation is the two rules of tic-tac-toe: the players alternate and three in a row wins. If the scientist could now examine all possible games of tic-tac-toe, he or she would find that this explanation covers all possible games.

It isn't necessary for a scientific law to be as cut-and-dried as this. Consider the following variant of tic-tac-toe: there are two jars, both filled with 9 marbles. One has all possible locations on a tic-tac-toe square, such as top row center or middle row right. The other has 6 marbles with X on them and 3 with O. The game (such as it is) is played by picking one marble from each jar and following the instructions: if the top row center marble and an X marble are picked, place an X in the center of the top row. The game is played until all squares are filled. Show enough of the games to a scientist (or an exceptionally well-programmed computer), and the rules will be deduced. Many important scientific laws are statistical; it is impossible to predict how every molecule in a jar filled with gas will move, but we can compute how the pressure will increase when the gas in the jar is heated (this is basically what happens with the tires on your car).

Even if we have to examine every possible tic-tac-toe game, if there are rules they can be deduced—and if there are no rules that can be deduced as well. A finite Universe differs from a tic-tac-toe game in that there are a lot more different pieces than just Xs and Os, and many more places to put them; but it's still finite, and the principles of the tic-tac-toe game apply.

Am I absolutely convinced that I'm right? No, but it makes a lot of sense to me. However, what I contend is that in an infinite Universe, there must be rules that we *cannot* deduce; and that's the key point in my argument.

"Jupiter—and Beyond, the Infinite"

One of the classic movies of my generation was *2001: A Space Odyssey,* a film version of a story, *The Sentinel*, by Arthur C. Clarke—this marks his third separate appearance in this book. *The Sentinel*[1] describes an expedition to the Moon that discovers an alien artifact. The humans who discover the artifact try to figure out what it is. The narrator of the story conjectures that it is a sort of motion sensor placed here by an alien culture. When the race of man is capable of traveling from the Earth to the Moon, it might be time for the alien race to pay them a visit.

The story ends here; the movie does not. The artifact receives a signal in the movie that originates from the general vicinity of Jupiter, so the humans build a spaceship to investigate. As the spaceship closes in on Jupiter, a screen caption reads, "Jupiter—and beyond, the infinite." It sounds good in the movie, but the infinite is WAY beyond Jupiter. In fact, the infinite is inconceivably far beyond Jupiter—and may not be a location at all! The infinite may simply be this: no matter how far you've gone, you can always go one step farther.

Pinning down the infinite has not been an easy task for mathematicians. The infinite appears most straightforwardly in counting, and so we'll turn our attention to that.

The most basic mathematical objects turn out to be extremely hard to define. For instance, we all know what a point is, and Euclid defined a point as that which has no part, by which he meant that there was nothing smaller than a point. However, what Euclid did here was to use the common understanding of what a point was, and then go from there. At some stage, we have to rely to some extent on common understanding.

This is especially true when it comes to the counting numbers. I think I learned to count when I was about three years old, and I've been teaching and studying mathematics ever since. However, if someone asked me to define "three," I couldn't do it! When we initially learn the idea and purpose of counting, we focus not on "three" but something I will call "three-ness," which is that property shared by any collection of three objects. Collections of three apples, or three cookies, or three dollars all have the property of "three-ness," as does a collection consisting of two apples and one cookie, or a collection of one apple, one cookie, and one dollar. We initially teach "three-ness" to children by drawing pictures of a collection of three apples and a collection of three cookies, and having the children draw lines which connect one apple to one cookie. In so doing, children learn the idea of what mathematicians call "one-to-one correspondence." Any collection of three objects can be put in one-to-one correspondence with any other collection of three objects. The property that all these collections of three objects have in common is what we refer to as "three."

This gives rise to the counting numbers: 1,2,3.... Later, children learn about 0, which is intrinsically a little harder to understand than 3, because it's hard to explain "zero-ness" by the same method that we explain "three-ness." This results in one of the initial arithmetic confusions teachers encounter—0 is not the same as *nothing*. *Nothing* is a contraction of "no thing"—no apples, no cookies, no dollars...no anything else, simultaneously. If we are talking about apples, 0 refers to no apples—0 is limited to the system under discussion.

However, once we have an understanding of what 0 means, we can form the system of natural numbers: 0,1,2,3.... This is a fundamental mathematical system, and so it should have a formal mathematical theory associated with it, in the same way that points and lines have Euclidean geometry. Even though the underlying principles of arithmetic have been well-known for millennia, it wasn't until the end of the 19th century that a good formal theory of arithmetic was produced. This theory is known as Peano arithmetic, after Giuseppe Peano, an Italian mathematician who did roughly the same thing for arithmetic that Euclid did for geometry: codify existing ideas and formalize them.

It won't hurt—much—to get an idea of Peano arithmetic. The objects under discussion are the natural numbers, but you can't really jump in with a definition of "57." You've got to start somewhere, and so the first axiom is that 0 is a natural number. This is analogous to Euclid's definition of "a point is that which has no part." Peano, like Euclid, had to start somewhere.

Peano had it easier than Euclid when it came to defining relationships between the objects of arithmetic. The only objects in arithmetic—at least, at this stage of the game—are the natural numbers. Euclid starts with BOTH points and lines. Furthermore, Peano only has to talk about equality between two natural numbers, what equality means. Euclid had a more difficult task because he had to discuss the idea of congruence, the concept that a line of length 3 between 2 points was somehow the same no matter where the 2 points were located.

It was also easier for Peano than Euclid when it came to the construction within the system of other objects. We know that we can put lines together to form figures: angles, polygons, intersecting lines, etc. These objects are more complex than the points and lines from which they are formed. However, if you put two natural numbers together—via addition—what you get is another natural number.

As a result, four of the axioms of Peano arithmetic are very easy to understand:

[1] 0 is a natural number.

[2] For every natural number, there is a next natural number. Intuitively, 57 is the next natural number after 56. "Next" is merely a way to say "add 1" without having to define addition to do it.

[3] 0 is not the next natural number of any natural number. Again, intuitively you understand that you can't add 1 to any natural number and get 0. It's impossible to add one more cookie to a pile of cookies and end up with no cookies. There are no "cookie monsters"—a cookie which eats all the other cookies and then, like the instructions in *Mission Impossible*, self-destructs.

[4] If two numbers have the same next number, they must be the same number. You can't add one to two different numbers and end up with the same number.

These axioms taken together produce infinitely many different natural numbers, because if we start with 0, the next number after 0 differs from 0, the next number after that differs from both 0 and the next number after 0, and so on. However, there is no guarantee that this process doesn't skip some of the numbers, and it would be a tragedy if this scheme failed to produce all the natural numbers.

In order to do this, Peano introduced another axiom, and in so doing unlocked Pandora's box:

> [5] If a collection of natural numbers contains 0 and contains the next number after any number in the collection, then the collection consists of all natural numbers.

You can see how this dispenses with the problem above, as this axiom guarantees that the above procedure (start with 0, take the next number after that, then the next number after that...) produces all the natural numbers. It looks innocuous, but it's extremely powerful, for it allows for an idea called the Principle of Mathematical Induction.

One of the best ways I know to introduce how the Principle of Mathematical Induction may be used is to tell a classic story about one of the giants of mathematics. Carl Friedrich Gauss was one of the most famous mathematicians of all time, and revealed his talents at an early age, when a schoolteacher asked his class to add up the numbers from 1 to 100. He expected this problem to keep his students busy for some time, but when he walked by Gauss' desk, he discovered that the boy had written 5,050 on his slate (that's what they used in the late 18th century), and that's the correct answer.

At an early age, Gauss had discovered that if you add all the numbers from 1 up through a number we'll denote by N, the answer is $N(N+1)/2$, so the sum of the numbers from 1 to 100 is $100 \times 101/2 = 5{,}050$. Gauss did this by a brilliant observation: he noticed that if you looked at pairs of numbers (1 and 100, 2 and 99, 3 and 98...) the sum of each pair was 101. There were 50 such pairs, the last being 50 and 51, so the sum of the numbers from 1 to 100 was $50 \times 101 = 5{,}050$. This same technique can be used to derive the formula for adding up all the numbers from 1 to N, but we'll get this result by using the Principle of Mathematical Induction. This is one of the few times we'll actually do any math in this book, and you can feel perfectly free to skip it by going to the paragraph that begins with the words "But how" on page 139.

In order to use axiom [5] in the form given, we have to modify the conjecture a little. Instead of computing the sum from 1 to N, we're going to compute the sum from 1 to N+1. The reason for doing this is that [5] requires us to have a set which contains 0, and the sum of the numbers from 1 to N, where N=0, doesn't make sense—we're adding up numbers going forward from 1, not backwards. However, if we add up the numbers from 1 to N+1, when N=0 we're adding up 1 through 0+1, which does make sense.

What would our conjecture look like? The expression N(N+1)/2 is just half the product of the last number being added with the next number after that. So, if we're adding up the numbers from 1 to N+1, the last number being added is N+1, the next number after that is N+2, and so the formula should be that the sum of the numbers from 1 through N+1 is (N+1) × (N+2)/2.

So, let S be the set of natural numbers (0, 1, 2, 3...) for which the conjecture is true; the conjecture being "the sum of 1 through N+1 is (N+1) × (N+2)/2". This set certainly contains 0, because the sum of 1 through 1 is just 1, and if we substitute N=0 into (N+1) × (N+2)/2, we get (0+1) × (0 + 2)/2 = 1 × 2/2 = 1. So the set S contains 0 (we could also say the formula is true for N=0; same thing).

We now need to show what is called the induction step: if S contains N, then S contains N+1. This requires a little algebra, which we include for completeness. If algebra troubles you, just skip to the end of the few equations that follow.

We need to show that the set S contains N+1, which is equivalent to showing that

1 + 2 + 3 + ... + (N +2) = ((N+2) + 1) × ((N+2)+2)/1. The expression on the right is just (N+3) × (N+4)/2.

But

1 + 2 + 3 + ... + (N+2) = (1+2+3 + ... + N+1) + (N+2) we just regrouped the expression on the left

= (N+1) × (N+2)/2 + (N+2) this is the assumption that S contains N

= (N+2) × ((N+1)/2 + 1) factoring out N+2

= (N+2) × (N+3)/2 because (N+1)/2+1 = (N+1)/2 + 2/2 = (N+3)/2

The last expression on the right is just half the last number being added times the next number after that, because the last number being added is N+2. This shows that the set S contains all natural numbers, and the formula can be relied upon to always be correct.

But how do mathematical patterns and the Peano Axioms relate to the real world?

That's the key question. Mathematical patterns often relate to the real world, and they need not necessarily be the ones that can be established by working with mathematical induction. Probably the most famous mathematical pattern is the one established for right triangles by Pythagoras some 2,500 years ago, that the square of the hypotenuse is equal to the sum of the squares of the two sides of the right triangle. This was established more than 2,000 years before Giuseppe Peano was born, and has proved tremendously useful for measuring and building—to say nothing of establishing the foundation on which trigonometry was constructed.

Geometry is a branch of mathematics for which there are practical applications. Physics, however, is not formally a branch of mathematics—it is a discipline which uses mathematics. There are lots of disciplines which use mathematics: architecture, banking, cooking, and a host of others. In fact, all these disciplines use arithmetic, but do they really need the Peano Axioms? In fact, do we really need the idea that the numbers are built upon the idea of a next number?

Is There Always a Next Number?

In the integers, yes. In the real world, maybe and maybe not. And that distinction is one of the key ideas in this book.

Let's consider cookies, which are often used to introduce children to many of the ideas of arithmetic. 1 + 2 = 3 is not initially learned in terms of numbers but in terms of cookies. If you give a child who has 1 cookie an additional 2 cookies, that child now has 3 cookies. Similarly, all the arithmetic operations are given as examples with cookies. 3 - 1 = 2 is learned as "if you take away 1 cookie from 3 cookies, 2 cookies are left." 2 × 3 = 6 is "2 groups of 3 cookies makes a total of 6 cookies." Finally, 6 ÷ 3 = 2 is learned as "if you share 6 cookies equally among 3 children, each child will receive 2 cookies."

I'm not sure when this tradition of teaching arithmetic with cookies began, but it's a very good way to do it. And, of course, all the usual rules of arithmetic remain in force for all the numbers of cookies (or anything else) a child is likely to encounter. Obviously, there is a limit to the number of cookies that a cookie jar, or the Earth, or the visible Universe, can contain. Whereas the size of the cookie jar may present some practical problems, there is always someplace else to store the additional cookies, and no one—not even the Cookie Monster—can accumulate every single cookie that the Earth can hold, to say nothing of the visible Universe. So the question of whether there is a next cookie is moot.

However, the question of whether there is a next number is not quite moot, because it bears upon the question of whether phenomena transcending natural laws can exist. And that brings us to logic.

Mathematics Gets Introspective

Mathematics is like architecture, both in terms of what it does on a case-by-case basis, and how it evolved as a discipline. Architecture first consisted of constructing individual buildings. However, after enough individual buildings had been constructed, people started developing general principles to be used in the construction of buildings. In order to develop these general principles, it was necessary to have some experience in constructing a variety of different types of buildings in order to come up with some general principles.

As the 19th century came to an end, mathematics took a look at what it had accomplished. There were some really impressive achievements, and mathematics had provided tools which enabled the development of the physical sciences and related technology. It had also provided tools for the social and life sciences, although those would be developed and expanded in the century to come. Formal mathematics, which had started with the geometry developed by the Greeks more than two millennia previously, had also started to develop the tools to examine mathematics itself.

The turn of a century is often a time of optimism, as it was at the turn of the most recent millennium—despite fears of an impending Y2K disaster. The 1890s had been a relatively peaceful period, known as "The Gay Nineties," and technology was starting to bring accelerated improvements to everyday life. Automobiles were starting to become a common mode of transportation, and the use of electricity was expanding man's ability to light his cities and communicate across long distances.

Mathematics, too, was in an optimistic frame of mind. The year 1900 featured a meeting in Paris of the International Congress of Mathematicians, a gathering of many of the world's finest mathematicians. Preeminent among these was the German mathematician David Hilbert, who laid out a road map at the conference for mathematics to travel in the coming century. Hilbert proposed 23 problems for mathematicians to tackle: problems whose solutions would enable great leaps forward in mathematics.[2] One problem in particular will command our attention: Hilbert's Second Problem was to prove that the axioms of arithmetic were consistent.

Consistent Axiom Systems

An axiom system is said to be consistent if, using that axiom system, it is impossible to prove that something is simultaneously true and false. Of course, we'd want to throw out any axiom system in which one could prove that something is simultaneously true and false, because if we could prove that one result was simultaneously true and false, how could we be sure that something we had previously proved true could not later also be proved false? Imagine, for instance, that the axioms of Euclidean geometry were shown to be inconsistent. All the results of geometric measurement that we use to help construct and understand our world would suddenly be open to doubt. Pythagoras proved that the square of the hypotenuse of a right triangle was equal to the sum of the squares of the other two sides. We accept his proof (and the hundreds of other proofs of the theorem, including one originally proposed by President Garfield)—and we have never found a right triangle for which this fails to be true. But what if there is one lurking out there?

Even more fundamental than geometry is arithmetic. Arithmetic underlies practically everything we do using numbers—and that's a lot of what we do. We'd better hope that the axioms of arithmetic are consistent. If they aren't, what's to prevent arithmetic from leading us astray in a critical area such as daily commerce?

No wonder Hilbert felt that proving the consistency of arithmetic was of critical importance. The problem, originally propounded in 1900, was still unsolved in 1930, when Hilbert attended a conference where he gave a talk entitled "Logic and the Understanding of Nature." Of course, if Nature is completely understandable, the concept of the supernatural becomes moot, so one can be pretty sure that Hilbert was not a big believer in supernatural phenomena. Hilbert ended his talk with the confident statement "We must know. We shall know."

Little did Hilbert realize at the time that at the same conference, an obscure Austrian mathematician was to deliver a paper that would not only dash Hilbert's dream, but would create what I consider to be a plausible explanation for the existence of supernatural phenomena in an infinite Universe.

Godel and the Incompleteness Theorem

How can the determination of whether arithmetic is consistent have any relation to the existence of supernatural phenomena?

Let's go back to the intuitive definition of what constitutes supernatural phenomena: things that happen that cannot be explained by science. It's not just enough to have a one-shot phenomenon that cannot be explained by science, such as an apparent miraculous victory by an underdog against a seemingly insuperable opponent. Things that happen by chance are not supernatural; chance is actually incorporated in several important theories from physics, notably statistical mechanics and quantum mechanics. Given enough time, even the most unlikely things will happen, as long as they are simply unlikely and not impossible.

No, in order to have something that we can safely classify as supernatural, we must have a repeatable phenomenon that transcends the laws of science. That's not to say that there aren't other supernatural occurrences which do not fall into this category, but they are not phenomena that are dealt with in this book.

Let's return to the example of the law of gravity in Asimov's story *Nightfall*. Gravity, as we know, is a relatively simple physical phenomenon—if we can consider as simple a physical law that took more than a century to unearth, from Copernicus' hypothesis that the planets revolve around the Sun to Newton's elucidation of the workings of gravity. It took longer on the *Nightfall* planet because of the extreme difficulty of working in an environment where six stars, rather than our single Sun, exerted their gravitational influence. But what if the law of gravity could be shown to transcend science?

There are several obvious problems here. How can one have a law that actually transcends science? Are there such laws? How can we know that such laws exist without actually establishing them? To find the answer to these questions, we have to go back to the conference at which David Hilbert, talking about the laws of Nature, said "We must know. We shall know."

A conference for mathematicians is one of the ways mathematicians exchange ideas. Even though publication was not a difficult matter in the 1930s, conferences afford mathematicians an opportunity to gather, present new ideas, and discuss them in order to obtain rapid feedback. Nowadays this can be accomplished by posting a paper on a Website devoted to mathematics, but back in the 1930s, rapid feedback was best obtained by delivering a paper at a conference to an audience of those mathematicians who might be interested in it, and then discussing it afterwards. Mathematicians are people too, and they enjoy the opportunity to get together with like-minded people and discuss interesting ideas in a congenial atmosphere. A lot of mathematics gets done in restaurants and bars. There are numerous stories, not all of which are apocryphal, about mathematicians convening at a restaurant, and having run out of available paper on which to write, start writing on the tablecloth.

At any rate, at the same conference where Hilbert was speaking on the laws of Nature, a lesser-known mathematician named Kurt Godel was delivering a paper whose implications were not initially realized by the few attendees who listened to his presentation. Godel was discussing the consistency of the Peano Axioms for arithmetic, which by then had become the industry standard for the axiomatic treatment of arithmetic. Godel proved a truly remarkable and unexpected result, which later became known as the First Incompleteness Theorem. Either the Peano Axioms were inconsistent, or it was possible to formulate what came to be known as undecidable propositions within the framework of arithmetic.

Undecidable Propositions

What is an undecidable proposition? An undecidable proposition is a true statement—about integers when we are referring to the Peano Axioms—which cannot be proven. In order to understand exactly what this means, we need to dig a little more deeply into how statements about integers are processed.

Let's consider a relatively simple statement: if N is an integer, then 2N+3 is an even number. We can immediately show that this statement is false, because if N=1, 2N+3 = 2 × 1 + 3 = 5, which is odd. So this statement is false. One possible way to show that a statement is false is to do what we just did: simply find a specific instance in which it is false.

It was relatively easy to show that this statement was false, because we only needed to look at the case where N=1 to find an example of when it was false. However, it is possible to imagine that in order to show that a statement is false, we might have to look at a relatively large collection of integers.

A prime number is one which is divisible only by itself and 1, 2, 3, 5, 7, 11, and 13 are examples of primes, but 4 is not prime, because it is divisible by 2. Suppose we consider the statement: for every integer n, the expression $N^2 + N + 41$ is prime. This statement is true for EVERY integer from 1 to 40 (you can check this if you want to), but it is false for N=41, because $41^2 + 41 + 41 = 1763 = 41 \times 43$.

Let's imagine that there is a statement about integers which is true for all the integers from 1 to 1,000,000,000,000,000,000,000 (one sextillion) but is false for 1,000,000,000,000,000,000,001. Even though no human could decide whether the statement is true by examining a sextillion cases, possibly a superfast computer could. At any rate, the rules of arithmetic encompass the ability to examine any *finite* number of integers in order to decide whether a statement is false. What the rules of arithmetic do *not* allow us to do is to examine *all* the integers one at a time to determine whether the statement is true or false. If we are to construct a proof, or find an example, we must do so by writing down a finite string of symbols, because such a string of symbols could be read, at least in theory, by a sufficiently fast reader or computer. Any string of symbols that is infinitely long could not be read, and so the rules determine that we can't go through "one integer at a time" checking to see that a statement is true or false.

Here's another paragraph you can skip if you don't want to be bothered with actual mathematics. Just because we can't go through all the integers one at a time doesn't mean that we can't prove or disprove statements that involve all integers. In addition to mathematical induction, there are lots of ways to prove statements. For instance, the fact that $(a+b)^2 = a^2 + 2ab + b^2$ (remember this from algebra?) can be proved simply by manipulating the rules for addition and multiplication. The fact that the sum of the powers of 2 from $2^0 = 1$ through 2^N equals $2^{N+1}—1$ can be seen by the following argument, familiar to anyone who watches March Madness (the annual college basketball championship). After the play-in games, there are $64 = 2^6$ teams remaining. If each game uses one basketball, how many are required for the tournament?

The final uses 1 basketball, the semi-finals (the Final Four) 2 basketballs, the quarterfinals (the Elite Eight) uses 4 basketballs, etc., so the total number of basketballs used is 1 + 2 + 4 + 8 + 16 + 32, which is the sum of the powers of 2 from $2^0 = 1$ through 2^5. If we imagine that the loser of each game receives the basketball as a consolation prize, the tournament continues until there is only one non-loser. Only one of the 64 teams will not receive a basketball, and so the sum of the powers of 2 from $2^0 = 1$ through 2^5 is $63 = 2^6—1$. Just expand March Madness to include 2^N teams, and you've proved the result. Maybe it isn't completely clear that this constitutes a formal proof as it stands, but it's always possible to translate a valid informal argument into a valid formal proof.

Godel constructed his example of a true statement which could not be proven by working from the problems incurred by self-referential statements. Here's the classic example of a self-referential statement, and the paradox that such statements sometimes involve. Consider the following four-word sentence: *This sentence is false.*

This four-word sentence distills what is known as the Paradox of Epimenides. It's a relative of the riddle from the Middle Ages: The barber shaves exactly those men in the village who do not shave themselves. Who shaves the barber?

The problem with both of these is that assuming it is either true or false enables one to conclude the opposite. In case this is causing you some headscratching, here's how it goes for the Paradox of Epimenides.

If the sentence is true, it is true that it is false. So it is false.

If the sentence is false, it is false that it is false. So it is true.

Similarly, back in the Middle Ages, they came up with the following circular reasoning.

If the barber does not shave himself, then, because the barber shaves every man who does not shave himself, the barber must shave the barber.

If the barber shaves himself, then he is violating the restriction that he shaves only those men who do not shave themselves. Thus, this hypothesis leads to a contradiction, and so either hypothesis leads to a contradiction.

It's the self-referential aspect of the sentence "This sentence is false" that causes the problem. The same situation occurs with regard to the problem with the barber.

Okay, I assume you're now willing to accept the fact that it is possible to construct English sentences which cannot be determined to be true or false. However, this isn't quite the same thing as finding an English sentence which is true, but cannot be shown to be true. This question is tied up with that "consistency of arithmetic" problem, because if you have true sentences that you can't prove are true, how do you know that they might not be false as well as being true? After all, since you can't prove they are true, and you can't check that they are true one integer at a time, couldn't they be false as well as true? This raises the following question: is it possible to construct true arithmetical sentences about numbers which cannot be determined to be true?

If you think this task is impossible, you are in good company. David Hilbert not only thought that this could not be done, he thought that one of the tasks of mathematicians would be to construct logical machinery such that, when the crank was figuratively turned, true theorems could be proven true and false ones proven false. What Godel did in essence was this: he demonstrated that either the Peano Axioms for arithmetic were inconsistent, or there were arithmetical sentences that could be constructed from the counting numbers which could neither be proved true or false. Now, absolutely nobody believes that the Peano Axioms are inconsistent—we've been working with arithmetic far too long and we've never come across an arithmetic statement that is both true and false. So there must be true arithmetic statements which cannot be proven to be true.

Godel actually constructed such an arithmetic statement, although the statement itself was probably not one would normally associate with what we think of as arithmetic. Godel described a method of assigning numbers to all possible arithmetic propositions; this is now called "Godel numbering." This really isn't so surprising by itself, because arithmetic propositions are just "sentences" of finite length using a fixed alphabet (the digits and the mathematical symbols). He then constructed a sentence involving the Godel numbers similar to "This sentence is false." Libraries have the Dewey Decimal System for numbering books as a rough analogue to Godel numbering for arithmetic sentences. The big difference is that if you look at the Dewey decimal number for a book, it may be able to tell you exactly what book it refers to, but it cannot tell you exactly what the book says. However, if you know the Godel number, you can construct the arithmetic sentence from it simply by knowing the number.

The result that either the Peano Axioms are inconsistent or that there are true arithmetic statements which cannot be proven to be true, is known as Godel's First Incompleteness Theorem. It is undoubtedly one of the most brilliant accomplishments of mathematics, in the 20th century or otherwise. I also think that it has significant consequences for the existence of supernatural phenomena—regular, repeatable phenomena which cannot be explained by science. I've taken a long while to get to the essence of this argument, but here it is in a nutshell, followed by an explanation. If we live in an infinite Universe, there must be copies of things that can be measured to which the counting numbers apply. These things may be distances (the Universe goes on forever in space), time (the

Universe goes on forever in time), mass (the Universe contains an infinite quantity of stuff—it could do that in a finite space if it contains things of arbitrarily high density), or some other form of physically measurable parameter. For the time being, though, let's just stick to basics such as length, time, and mass, because quantities such as force, energy, momentum are all simple expressions compounded from the basic elements of length, mass, and time.

Any such system to which the counting numbers apply is subject to Godel's Incompleteness Theorem. That means that there are arithmetical sentences involving the quantities in these systems which are true but which we cannot determine that they are true. Unlike Einstein's equation $E = mc^2$, which we have determined to the best of our ability to be true, or the equation $E = mc^3$, which can easily be shown to be false via experiment, these sentences may never be known to us. They would be laws governing the systems they describe, such as energy, force, momentum, or whatever, which would express true mathematical relationships between measurable parameters and which could not be shown to be true. I submit that such laws would describe supernatural phenomena: regular, repeatable phenomena which would be beyond the power of science to confirm.

Even if by some chance one of these laws were revealed to us—after all, some scientist might "get lucky" and guess the form of a law—we would never be able to determine whether or not it was true. This may strike you as rather weird; if you see the law, how would you be unable to determine whether or not it is true? This may not be a common situation in astronomy, chemistry, or physics, but it is fairly common in mathematics, where difficult conjectures abound. There have been examples where conjectures that have stood for centuries finally succumbed to analysis. A recent example was the proof by Andrew Wiles of Fermat's Last Theorem, which was originally propounded in the 17th century and did not finally fall until 1997.

There have also been examples of problems which have been shown to be undecidable. The first one, in which Godel did something for arithmetic similar to what the Paradox of Epimenides did for true and false, was highly artificial, it would never come up in the real world and was constructed solely for the purpose of exhibiting an undecidable proposition. Several problems that have come up in advanced mathematics have actually been shown to be undecidable and aren't appropriate for discussion here. However, there are two problems which are currently sitting on the fence as far as undecidability goes, and they're pretty easy to understand.

- **The Goldbach Conjecture**. Every even number is the sum of two prime numbers. For example, the even number 84 is the sum of the two prime numbers 41 and 43. This conjecture has been in existence for almost 300 years, and is probably the oldest unsolved problem in mathematics. (It took over this position after Wiles established Fermat's Last Theorem.)

  Mathematicians have been nibbling away at the edges of the Goldbach Conjecture, and some think that they can see the light at the end of the tunnel, indicating that the Conjecture is true, or the darkness, indicating that it is false. What they hope not to see is the fog of undecidability, because the Conjecture is so well known and so venerable. However, here's one that mathematicians feel may be shrouded in the fog of undecidability.

- **The Collatz Conjecture**. Pick a number, any number. If it is even, divide it by 2. If it is odd, triple it and add 1. Take the result, apply the same rules depending upon whether the result is odd or even, and keep going. Let's say we started with 11. Here's what happens:

  Step 1. 11 is odd, so $3 \times 11 + 1 = 34$.

  Step 2. 34 is even, so $34/2 = 17$.

> Continuing, we obtain 11,34,17,52,26,13,40,20,10,5,16, 8,4,2,1. The Collatz Conjecture is that no matter what number you start with, you eventually end up with 1.

Here's why each of these problems is exceedingly difficult. If the Peano Axioms are consistent, according to Godel there are only three possible choices for any proposition: it could be true and provable, it could be undecidable (true but incapable of being proven true), or it could be false (which could be demonstrated simply by showing the right counterexample).

If you're a mathematician who has decided to work on one of these problems, you face the following difficulties. If you try to establish that it is true, you know that lots of other mathematicians have tried and failed. If it is undecidable and you try to establish that it is true, you're "drawing dead," as it can't be done. So you decide that you're going to try to find a counterexample.

To find a counterexample to the Goldbach Conjecture, you'd simply have to find an even number which is *not* the sum of two primes. The catch here is that, as numbers get larger, it gets harder and harder to determine whether or not they are primes. As a result, if I were to write down a 1,000-digit number that ended in 4 (so that you would know it was even), it's unlikely that we would know all the primes less than that number, and so that's more work for you to do.

To find a counterexample to the Collatz Conjecture, even though all you have to do is take numbers and divide them by 2, or multiply them by 3 and add 1, how can you determine that you're on a path that will continue forever?

I'd be surprised if anyone who reads this book takes a shot at either the Goldbach Conjecture or the Collatz Conjecture. Because, as far as I know, this book is the first place where the possibility of undecidable propositions using the basic constructs of mass, length, and time has been proposed as a possible source of supernatural phenomena, I felt it was worthwhile to discuss two possibly undecidable propositions in the simple realm of integers to get a sense of how difficult it might be to come up with undecidable propositions in the more complex realm of physics. The reason that the realm of physics is more complex than the realm of mathematics—at least, in this case—is that there are other axioms from physics that must be incorporated along with the Peano Axioms.

Although I can't see how the possible undecidability of the Goldbach Conjecture might have any physical ramifications, I can see a faint possibility for an idea related to the Collatz Conjecture. Nuclear fission is the process of breaking the nucleus of an atom into smaller pieces, whereas nuclear fusion is the process of combining smaller nuclei into bigger ones. Not all types of fission and fusion are possible; there are rules that are arithmetic in nature which determine the types of fission and fusion reactions that can take place. A far-out possibility (somewhere between Jupiter and the infinite, but a lot closer to the latter) is that discovering that the Collatz Conjecture is undecidable may mean that one cannot determine what will happen in a sequence of fission-fusion reactions.

There's an elephant in the room, and we can't ignore it. Are there reasonable candidates out there among phenomena which are conventionally thought of as supernatural which might possibly be supernatural in the sense that this book proposes?

I realize that if I've trodden on thin ice up to this point, speculation along these lines is ice so thin it would have difficulty supporting the weight of a gnat. Nonetheless, later in this book, I'm going to give it a try.

8 The Baloney Detector

So the argument that I propose for the existence of supernatural phenomena is this: in an infinite Universe, there must be scientific laws—mathematical expressions involving the measurable parameters of physics—which are true but can never be validated. The first thing we need to check is whether there are any obvious flaws in the argument. Unfortunately, this theory is not like Einstein's Theory of Relativity in the sense that there is a physical experiment we can do to check if its predictions are consistent with reality. It's a little more like the string theory description of the Universe, but even the string theory description of the Universe makes predictions that we might be able to test someday. So, for the moment, let's run the argument presented here through a baloney detector, and we happen to have a really good one available, thanks to Carl Sagan's *The Demon-Haunted World.*

In that book, Sagan proposes examining an argument with a baloney detector[1]—a gauntlet of techniques designed to expose erroneous and specious arguments. Let's see how this argument stands up to Sagan's baloney detector. The baloney detector consists of two parts—checking on the facts themselves, and the interpretation of the facts.

Seek Independent Confirmation of the Facts

This isn't so easy, because what I propose is a theory. The only checkable fact that I can see is that Godel's Impossibility Theorem states that any consistent axiomatic system including the integers contains undecidable propositions. This has been an accepted part of mathematics for nearly 80 years.

However, it wouldn't be a theory worth wasting any time on unless the other part of the assumption—that the Universe was infinite—was at least worthy of consideration. I know of several prominent physicists who have expressed this opinion on TV. I recently heard Professor Michio Kaku, who hosts a number of highly popular TV shows on science, expound the view that he believes in what he called "continuing genesis" in the Multiverse. Professor Alan Guth, who developed the remarkable theory of the inflationary Universe that is now an integral part of the standard model, also believes it. I believe it, too. I don't know what portion of scientists believe it, but I'd love to see the results of a survey.

Finally, I think that John Archibald Wheeler also believed it. Wheeler, as well as other physicists, spent some time investigating a possible connection between the Heisenberg Uncertainty Principle (we'll discuss this later when we talk about quantum mechanics) and the Godel Impossibility Theorem. He didn't find one, but Wheeler was a brilliant physicist, and I'm sure he was aware that the Godel Impossibility Theorem talks about axiom schemes incorporating the Peano Axioms, which involve the integers, an infinite set. Although it is possible that Wheeler might have been searching for approximations in a finite Universe, I think it is more likely that he believed in an infinite Universe. Otherwise, why would he be spending time on Godel's Impossibility Theorem, which does not apply to finite sets?

Encourage Debate

I would absolutely love to hear knowledgeable scientists debate this. In fact, my hope is that this book will encourage such debates. I also hope that it will encourage further investigation.

Although the tenure system in universities often comes under attack, and although as a tenured professor I am a beneficiary of such a system, I believe society is a beneficiary of this system as well. The tenure system frees those who have acquired tenure to investigate questions that may not necessarily have an immediate payoff. Although a lot of these investigations lead nowhere, some have led to incalculable benefits for society—and would almost certainly have been scrubbed by most corporations for lack of an immediate payoff.

Frederick Sanger is one of a bare handful of individuals who won have won two Nobel Prizes; both of his were in chemistry. The first was for determining the structure of insulin; this took him 11 years. He was among the first to work out the DNA sequencing techniques which play such an important role in biology and medicine today; this led to his second Nobel Prize. Sanger was free to do work that did not have an immediate payoff in the quarterly report of a company, and the world is substantially the richer for it. Much of today's biotechnology industry is a direct outgrowth of Sanger's pioneering efforts.

I don't think the fact that the paranormal and supernatural are looked on with disdain by the scientific community is the result of an *a priori* prejudice. Rather, it is a reflection of the fact that there are no solid results in the field and a lot of time and effort have been wasted upon it. It also doesn't help that there is a lot of contamination due to fraud. Nonetheless, it wouldn't take much time and effort to either expose a critical error I may have made, or to decide whether there is something here worth thinking about.

Avoid Arguments From Authority

I certainly haven't proposed this idea because I think Godel was a brilliant logician, or because a number of scientists believe in an infinite Universe. I've proposed this idea because it makes sense to me, and I'm putting my reasoning on the table for examination. Let the chips fall where they may.

I recently saw a bumper sticker which said, "The Bible says it. I believe it. That settles it." Science can never advance if it bases its conclusions on the word of an authority, whether that authority be God or Godel. It is true that there is often a prevailing paradigm in a scientific discipline, which is generally the result of demonstrable progress in a particular area. Certain lines of investigation have borne fruit, and these lines of investigation, and the theories they support, represent the prevailing paradigm. When the weight of scientific opinion is on a particular side, that often determines such important matters as where grant money goes. If you were trying to track down the cure for a particular disease, and you had money to award for research on that disease, you'd be more likely to award that money to pursue results in an area that had been successful than to risk that money on an unproven hypothesis.

Science is not "down" on the supernatural and the paranormal because it doesn't fit in with the preconceptions of scientists. It's because it hasn't borne any fruit, and very few scientists (outside of Josephson) have lines of investigation that they feel will bear fruit. Science was "down" on Salk's live-virus theory and Wegener's theory of continental drift. The live-virus theory and the theory of continental drift won adherents because they proved themselves. If the supernatural or paranormal can do that, they will win adherents as well.

Investigate Alternative Hypotheses

Well, there is an alternative hypothesis: the Universe is finite and all the laws of science can be discovered—at least in principle. I think this is a reasonable hypothesis. I don't know whether we will ever discover which of the two competing hypotheses, finite or infinite Universe, is true, but I'd absolutely love to know this. I think most other scientists would as well.

Don't Fall in Love With Your Own Theories

Oops. I'm in love with this theory—but I'm not so in love with it that I would reject any logical argument that would convince me that my reasoning is wrong (although I am sufficiently in love with it that I'd try like hell to find holes in the argument). I'm also not so in love that I would reject solid evidence in favor of a finite Universe. The truth is that I'm not in a position to make the call as to whether something constituted solid evidence; I'll leave that to the physicists and accept their judgment.

Express Arguments Quantitatively

It's certainly possible that somebody may think I've failed to do this, but in mathematics, finite and infinite are both extremely well-defined ideas. The big question here is the acceptance of the infinite as a quantity, but it's common mathematical practice. It's also accepted to a large extent in the sciences. For one thing, there has been a great deal of work on learning the eventual fate of the Universe, and that's certainly a question involving infinite time, even if the answer is "everything eventually stops—even the passage of time."

There is also a theory that although the Universe could be finite in the spatial and material sense, it could be infinite in the temporal sense. This theory requires that there be enough mass in the Universe for gravity to bring it all back together, in a reverse of the

Big Bang that is known as the Big Crunch. There are theories that this has already happened many times before, with the Universe exploding in a Big Bang, contracting in a Big Crunch, then exploding in another Big Bang, then contracting in another Big Crunch, and so on unto eternity. Although there are some recent developments (which will be discussed in Chapter 12) that make this appear unlikely, I haven't heard that this theory has been given the heave-ho.

Is the Hypothesis Capable of Being Falsified?

This is the criterion that is currently accepted for deciding whether an explanation is scientific. As we have noted, creationism is rejected as a scientific explanation because there is simply no way to falsify it.

Cosmological theories sometimes stumble here. In fact, I have heard scientists refer to some possibly unprovable theories as "mathematical theology." Currently, one of the leading candidates for an alternative to the standard model is a theory which posits an 11-dimensional Universe, 10 spatial dimensions and one time dimension.[2] We only see three spatial dimensions—up-down, left-right, front-back. Where did the other seven go? The theory holds that these dimensions are "compactified," so tiny in extent that we never see them, in the same way that a wire, which is a long three-dimensional cylinder, looks like a one-dimensional line when seen from a distance.

So why is this theory deemed scientific when creationism is not? The same theorists who espouse an 11-dimensional Universe are working on ways to test the theory, and it has an internally consistent mathematical description, which to some extent satisfies the requirement that the theory be quantifiable. Creationists see creationism as an alternative to evolution and point out what they see as flaws in the explanation given by evolution, but there are as yet no ways to falsify creationism.

Frankly, I don't see how to falsify the theory I propose, but I do see at least one way to supply confirming evidence, and possibly a second. There are known examples in mathematics of undecidable propositions (at least, granted the assumption that one is working in a consistent axiomatic system which incorporates the Peano Axioms). It may be possible to come up with an undecidable proposition in a model for an axiomatic system using physical parameters. That seems to me like a long shot, but until someone actually proves that this is not possible, I see it as basically the same type of obstacle faced by the 11-dimensional Universe theory. I don't know if this is possible, but it certainly seems to me that we're much closer to being able to do this now than the scientists of the 18th century were to understanding radioactivity. The scientists of the 18th century (and most of the 19th) didn't even know there was such a phenomenon as radioactivity.

There may be another way to demonstrate that we do live in an infinite Universe. I don't see this as being done directly, but by obtaining experimental results that could not be obtained in a finite Universe.

An Argument Is Only as Strong as Its Weakest Link

The argument is relatively simple, and there are only two links. The first is the assumption that the Universe is infinite, either in space or in time. This is an assumption that has been looked at in several different ways, and will be examined in some detail in Chapter 10.

The second is the assumption that, given an infinite Universe, there are mathematical expressions involving measurable parameters that can never be validated. I think that's a consequence of Godel's Impossibility Theorem, but I can understand if someone might say, "So what?" When I talked about Einstein's equation $E = mc^2$, I said that this could never be validated either. All we could do is perform experiments which, when taken all in all, would enable us to reach the conclusion that it was extremely unlikely that the equation was false.

This is certainly a reasonable statement, but I don't think it's a reasonable objection. Let's return to the idea, discussed earlier in the book, that there are three types of facts about the Universe: the known, the unknown, and the unknowable. It is the unknowable facts that are the ones that are of most interest, at least from the standpoint of this book, because those are the ones that could be classified as undecidable propositions.

How Much Is Unknowable?

There is no telling which of the unknown facts we will unearth in the future, but given enough time and scientists of sufficient talent, we could possibly discover any of them. That's why they are merely unknown. Yes, we might stumble over an unknowable fact, just as mathematicians have discovered specific undecidable propositions, but there is the real possibility that some unknowable facts are destined to remain forever hidden.

It is quite possible that, if the Universe is infinite, almost all of the facts about the Universe are unknowable. There are actually a number of precedents for this from mathematics. At about the time of Pythagoras, it was felt that all numbers were rational—either whole numbers such as 3, or fractions such as 11/4. One of the astounding discoveries of that era was the discovery of irrational numbers, numbers which were neither whole numbers nor fractions. The mathematicians of that era established that the square root of 2, which was the length of the hypotenuse of a right triangle whose sides were both equal to 1, could not be a rational number. This knowledge was felt to have the potential to disrupt society (hard to believe, but possibly society was a lot more fragile then), and so this knowledge was kept from the *hoi polloi* for some time.

Jump forward a couple of millennia. Mathematicians discovered that, in a sense that could be made specific, almost all real numbers were irrational—the familiar numbers such as 3 and 11/4 were merely an infinitesimal drop in the bucket when compared with the vastness of the irrational numbers. This situation has recurred several times in the development of mathematics. It takes a long time to discover an example of an irregular object, such as an irrational number, and later it is discovered that the vast majority of objects under consideration are irregular.

I'm a neophyte when it comes to mathematical logic, so I decided to pose the question "Is it possible that most propositions are undecidable?" to several mathematical logicians of my acquaintance. I was rather surprised to learn that none of the people that I asked had ever heard of anyone even considering the question. There's a reason for that; the way to decide the question of "almost all" comes from fields of mathematics that are somewhat distant from mathematical logic. At any rate, a couple of the people that I asked thought a) that it was an interesting question, b) that I should do some work to try to answer it (lots of luck to that one), and c) that it was indeed very possible.

How Did We Get So Lucky?

If almost all the facts about the Universe are unknowable, there are some interesting consequences. It means almost all the truths of the Universe are supernatural, in the sense that they will forever transcend scientific verification. It also adds a certain amount of force to what is referred to as the Anthropic Principle.[3] In cosmology, the Anthropic Principle is that the Universe is the way it is in order to accommodate conscious life (us). By this we mean that the physical constants of the Universe are such that conscious life can emerge. My favorite example of such a constant is the efficiency of hydrogen fusion, the nuclear process that powers the stars. If hydrogen fusion were about 15 percent less efficient than it is, it would be impossible for stars to create heavy elements, and the Universe would consist mostly of hydrogen. There would be no oxygen, and so there would be no water. If hydrogen fusion were about 15 percent more efficient than it actually is, hydrogen would fuse to helium so quickly that there wouldn't be enough free hydrogen around to form appreciable quantities of water. The Anthropic Principle states that this isn't just dumb luck; the Universe had to be this way because we, who need water, are here.

Considering that we have only seriously been in the science business for less than four centuries, we've made some truly amazing discoveries; we'll outline a few of the relevant ones at the beginning of the next chapter. How lucky are we that the discoveries we've made, which have had a revolutionary impact on our lives, were so accessible? The Laws of Mechanics and Universal Gravitation, the theory of electromagnetism, the laws of thermodynamics and the atomic theory (which underlies all of chemistry) are not undecidable propositions and inaccessible to our investigation. Profound though all of these are, they are (relatively speaking) low-hanging fruit on the Tree of All Scientific Laws—if, indeed, most of these laws were inaccessible to us. If I were an adherent of the Anthropic Principle, I would consider this to be supporting evidence; not only is the physical Universe the way it is because we are here, the intellectual Universe is as well.

9 Marital Telepathy

The story you are about to read is true. Only the identities of the participants have been changed.

The Centerville Surveys

Centerville is an average town in the United States, and is often used for conducting surveys. Because the inhabitants are generally busy people, the pollsters who work in Centerville have gotten in the habit of simply asking questions which can be answered YES or NO, rather than questions that require a rating "on a scale from 1 to 10."

As pollsters do, they tabulate the results of their polls, and because married couples form an important demographic, they look at how married couples answer their questions. In tabulating the results, the pollsters noticed two curious features that stood out.

1. If one were to ask *just one* question of a husband and *just one* question of a wife, no matter what the questions were, they would get agreement

half the time (both answering YES or both answering NO), and disagreement the other half the time (one answering YES and one answering NO). For instance, if pollsters were to walk into every home in Centerville and ask the husband *just one* question about sports that could be answered YES or NO and ask the wife *just one* question about fashion that could be answered YES or NO, the answers would agree half the time and disagree the other half. Okay, that may not strike you as very strange. If the husband and wife were answering questions by flipping a fair coin and answering YES if the coin landed heads and NO if the coin landed tails, they would agree half the time, because there are four possible ways the coins could land.

Husband's Coin	Wife's Coin	Agree or Disagree
Heads	Heads	Agree
Heads	Tails	Disagree
Tails	Heads	Disagree
Tails	Tails	Agree

Because each of the four possible arrangements above are equally likely, they agree in 2 out of 4 cases, half the time, and disagree the other half of the time. So the first feature wasn't so surprising.

2. This feature was an eye-opener. If you asked the *same* question of a husband and wife, they *always* agreed on their answer! Now husbands and wives often agree; that is not only one of the items that leads to people getting married, it's often the result of getting married. As time goes by, they tend to see more eye-to-eye on issues. But on *every* issue?

Searching for an explanation for this phenomenon, two possibilities were suggested. The first was that the husbands and wives were in telepathic contact with each other. If they were asked different questions, they would act independently, but if they were asked the same question the second person to be asked would know how the other answered and would make sure to agree with them. This would certainly be consistent with the fact that being asked the same question would result in 100-percent agreement.

However, another possibility was suggested that did not involve telepathy. It occurred to the pollsters that each couple had decided on a "secret rule" that only they would know on how to answer questions.

What would be an example of a secret rule? One possibility was that they agreed to answer all questions YES. That's a pretty simple secret rule. Another example of the same type of secret rule would be if that they had decided to answer all questions NO. However, if *every* married couple in Centerville had this type of secret rule, then the data would show 100-percent agreement between husband and wife for *every* question. That wasn't what the data showed; husbands and wives only gave the same answer 50 percent of the time.

So if each couple had evolved a secret rule, it had to have some degree of sophistication. Some questions would be answered YES and some questions would be answered NO. But the inhabitants of Centerville were old-fashioned; they were more than willing to answer questions about sports or politics or fashion, but they kept quiet about details concerning their marital life.

Pollsters puzzled over this for some time. Then someone thought of an extremely ingenious way to determine whether each couple had a secret rule—*without needing to know what that secret rule was!*

It's time for another appearance of Irving the Explainer, and you may not want to hear from him. If not, you can skip ahead to the paragraph that begins "Can you think..." on page 170. But if you'd like to know what this extremely ingenious way was, Irving is happy to tell you.

Here's how the pollsters went about it. They decided to construct a poll consisting of three questions. The first question was "Do you believe in ghosts?" The second question was "Do you think the legal voting age should be raised from 18 to 21?" The third question was "Do you believe people spend too much time on Facebook?" However, they decided to ask *only one* of those three questions of each husband and wife, and that each pollster would choose the question he or she would ask at random. This could be done by rolling a die just before asking the question: if the die showed 1 or 2, they would ask the ghost question, if it showed 3 or 4 they would ask the voting age question, and if it showed 5 or 6 they would ask the Facebook question.

There were nine different possible ways to ask one question each of husband and wife. The husband could be asked the ghost question and the wife could be asked any of the three questions—this would account for three possible ways. There were three more if the husband was asked the voting age question and three more if the husband was asked the Facebook question—a total of nine different ways.

However, let's suppose that each husband-wife pair had evolved a secret rule. There are a total of eight different ways that the secret rule could result in answers to the three questions. These are:

Ghost Question	Voting Age Question	Facebook Question
YES	YES	YES
YES	YES	NO
YES	NO	YES
YES	NO	NO
NO	YES	YES
NO	YES	NO
NO	NO	YES
NO	NO	NO

Remember, the pollsters have decided to ask *just one* question of the husband and *just one* question of the wife. If the husband and wife had a secret rule which resulted in *either* all YESes (row 1) or all NOs (row 8), no matter what question the pollsters asked of each, they would always agree. For example, if the husband and wife had a secret rule which resulted in a YES answer to all questions, each would answer YES no matter what question arose, and the answers would always agree.

If you take a look at rows 2 through 7, they have this in common: there are either two YESes and one NO, or one YES and two NOs. The calculation you will see next always comes up with the same result no matter which of rows 2 through 7 is the result of the secret rule. To illustrate, let's suppose that we look at a husband and wife whose secret rule, whatever it is, results in a YES to the ghost question, and NO to the voting age question and the Facebook question. This is row 4. This won't make any difference to the final results; once you see what happens in this case, you could check the other five possibilities (rows 2, 3, 5, 6, and 7), but it's not worth the effort unless you're really skeptical.

As I've mentioned, there are nine different ways the pollsters could randomly ask questions of husband and wife. I'll list the complete table with the nine different ways, under the assumption that both husband and wife answer YES to the ghost question and NO to each of the other two questions.

	Husband Question	Wife Question	Husband Answer	Wife Answer
1	Ghost	Ghost	YES	YES
2	Ghost	Voting Age	YES	NO
3	Ghost	Facebook	YES	NO
4	Voting Age	Ghost	NO	YES
5	Voting Age	Voting Age	NO	NO
6	Voting Age	Facebook	NO	NO
7	Facebook	Ghost	NO	YES
8	Facebook	Voting Age	NO	NO
9	Facebook	Facebook	NO	NO

Notice that the husband and wife agree in five cases out of nine (lines 1, 5, 6, 8 and 9). If you construct this table for the other five possibilities as described above, the husband and wife will *always* agree five times out of nine. So, if the husband and wife have a "secret rule" for answering questions, the data will show that they agree *at least* five times out of nine—as long as they are each randomly asked separate questions, and each question is asked one-third of the time. They will agree *every* time if they always have the same answer to each question (all YESes or all NOs), and they will agree 5 times out of 9 if they have a rule that either results in two YESes and one NO—or two NOs and one YES.

As we know, that's *not* what happened, because the first curious feature the pollsters noticed was that husbands and wives agreed half the time—not at least five times out of nine. The conclusion that the pollsters reached was that there was no secret rule for answering questions.

Can you think of an explanation other than telepathy which results in both Curious Feature #1 and Curious Feature #2? If you can, there's a good chance that there's a Nobel Prize in your future! I wasn't lying when I said that only the identity of the participants had been changed. As I'm sure you realize, the town of Centerville is an invention, but the situation described above is an exact parallel with one in real life—except that the pollsters aren't people involved in taking a survey, and the husbands and wives aren't people, either. The analogue of husbands and wives are known as "entangled photons," and the pollsters are physicists conducting an experiment to demonstrate one of the subtlest of quantum-mechanical phenomena.

Entanglement

Let's take a brief look at the physical phenomenon from quantum mechanics that motivated this problem. A photon is a particle with electromagnetic properties, one of which is the direction in which it spins around an axis. This is analogous to a child spinning a top. If a child grasps the top with the thumb and forefinger of the right hand he or she will spin the top in a clockwise direction, whereas if the top is grasped with the thumb and forefinger of the left hand, the top will be spun in a counterclockwise direction. Photons are a little like tops; they can spin about an axis.

When a calcium atom absorbs energy and later releases it so that it has the same amount of energy as before it absorbed the extra energy, it emits two photons. The spins of these photons are correlated in much the same way as the husband-wife answers to the same question was correlated in the Centerville survey. Once you knew how one member of a married couple answered the question, you would automatically know how the other member answered the question.

The situation for the two photons emitted by the calcium atom is exactly the same. Once you found out which direction one of the two photons spin, you know that the other will spin in the same direction. The term that's used to describe this arrangement is that the spins of the two photons are entangled.

Maybe this doesn't strike you as surprising, but it's stranger than it may appear at first sight. Instead of imagining that the husband and wife are being asked questions in the same house, imagine that one was being interviewed in New York and one was being interviewed in Los Angeles, and neither knew in advance what the question was going to be. It gets a little weird here, but maybe not so much that it disturbs you. So let's imagine that the husband and wife were being asked questions at the opposite ends of the Universe! The experimental analogy is that the spins of the two photons are being measured at the same time on opposite ends of the Universe—separated by almost 14 billion light years. The photons have no way to communicate with each other. Indeed, even if an elaborate communication scheme had been hatched by our two "anthropomorphic" photons, or by the husband and wife, it would be useless—no communication can travel faster than light. That's a limit that has never been violated in our Universe. So the question arises: how does one photon know how the other one will answer the question "In which direction are you spinning?" Could there be some hidden connection between the two photons that experiments are unable to determine?

Now we're entering the realm of something that might be a legitimate candidate for a supernatural phenomenon. In fact, the great physicist Albert Einstein actually labeled it as such, stating that this constituted "spooky [his word] action at a distance." [1] So disturbed by this phenomenon was Einstein that in 1935 he and two other physicists, Boris Podolsky and Nathan Rosen, described the situation above, in what has come to be known as the Einstein-Podolsky-Rosen experiment.[2] It's a thought experiment, meaning that it has never been performed, but the idea is basically the one described in the previous paragraph. Two groups of physicists, separated by vast distances, measure the spins of two entangled photons at the same time. There is no way for the photons to communicate with each other—at least, no way that does not involve faster-than-light communication, which violates everything we know about the Universe. Nothing moves faster than light. You might say, "Well, we don't know anything that moves faster than light—yet. But someday we'll discover something." That's possible, but highly unlikely. All sorts of ingenious equipment has been devised to test this hypothesis, and all sorts of measurements from physics, astronomy, and chemistry confirm it. It's not just highly unlikely, it's unlikely bordering on impossible.

Nonetheless, it doesn't stretch credibility too much to imagine that the problem is that there is something the experimenters are not measuring which determines how the photons both have the same spin. The analogue of this in the situation with the pollsters is the "secret rule"—something that the pollsters cannot deduce. The photon analogy of the "secret rule"—the variables that the experiments are not measuring—is known as the "hidden variables" hypothesis. No less a physicist than Albert Einstein himself endorsed the hidden variables hypothesis as the way to explain the "spooky action at a distance" that entanglement seemed to require.

An Astounding Discovery

As of the early 1960s, no one had come up with a satisfactory explanation for entanglement, but the hidden variables hypothesis was a leading contender. In fact, between the years 1935 and 1964, more than 100 scientific papers were written discussing the hidden variables hypothesis—some supporting it, some opposing it. However, in 1964, the Irish physicist John Bell came up with an experiment which would enable the hidden variables hypothesis to be tested.[3] This, after all, is one of the most important functions of science, to discover ways that competing explanations can be subjected to tests in the real world. Hopefully, when that is done, the true explanation will emerge.

What Bell did was little short of extraordinary. He discovered a way to prove that no hidden variables could exist, without even knowing what those variables might be! That's exactly what was described when the three-question scenario was presented earlier.

Bell's hypothetical experiment was a variation of the three-question scenario described in the Centerville survey. It also involved asking one of three possible questions of the photons that emerged from the calcium atom. If you think of a helicopter in midair, there are three perpendicular directions in which it can move: left or right, forward or backward, up or down. Left-right and forward-backward are determined by the direction in which the pilot is facing; up-down is relative to the surface of the Earth. A rubber ball on the floor can also be spun clockwise or counterclockwise relative to either the up-down axis, or you could give it topspin or underspin in either the forward-backward direction (spin around the left-right axis) or the left-right direction (that's a spin around the forward-backward direction). The three questions were 1) "Which way are you spinning about the left-right axis?" 2) "Which way are you spinning about the forward-backward axis?" and 3) "Which way are you spinning about the up-down axis?" As the photons emerge from the calcium atom, the experimenters can randomly choose to measure the spin around an axis as determined by any one of these directions.

Just as the pollsters separately and randomly chose questions to ask of husband and wife, the two groups of experimenters separately and randomly chose the axis around which they would measure the direction of the spin of the photons. And just as the husband and wife always came up with the same answer to the same question, no matter whether they were both asked the ghost question, the voting age question, or the Facebook question, the two entangled photons always exhibited the same spin direction whenever the experimenters chose to measure the spins of the two photons around the same axis.

Similarly, the data for the physical experiment should show that, as long as a random axis for checking spin is selected for each of the two emerging photons, if there are any hidden variables which determine spin direction, the two photons should spin in the same direction at least five times out of nine. That didn't happen. As was the case with the Centerville husbands and wives, the photons always spun in the same direction when the same axis was used.

When Bell proposed this experiment in 1964, the technology was not yet available to perform the experiment and obtain definitive answers. Although the spins could be measured, it was necessary to do so in such a way as to make sure that information could not be transmitted from one photon to the other, as ludicrous as this possibility seemed. That meant that it was necessary to conduct the experiments on the two separate photons so that light could not travel from one photon to the other in the time interval between the two experiments. That would ensure that no information about the results of the experiment could be communicated between photons.

Within 20 years, the technology had improved to the point that this could be done. It was first performed by the French physicist Alain Aspect; since then the experiment has been conducted many times.[4] The results are in and they are definitive. The photons spin in the same direction half the time. They do not spin in the same direction the more than five times in nine that would be required if there were hidden variables.

What Does It All Mean?

Physicists haven't yet decided what the absence of a hidden variables explanation for entanglement means at the deepest level of understanding. What they have done is to describe the situation by saying that a "local" theory—one which requires that an event that happens in one place cannot simultaneously influence an event that happens elsewhere—is inadequate to characterize physics. It's not supernatural—after all, it's part of Nature and that's the opposite of supernatural—but it is bizarre and counterintuitive.

There is a lesson to be learned from this with regard to the search for the supernatural. Recall that we are searching for secret rules of Nature, patterns in which the objects and forces that comprise the natural world remain hidden from science. After all, that's the intuitive idea of what constitutes supernatural phenomena, things that happen in a regular fashion that science is incapable of explaining.

What the absence of a hidden variables explanation for entanglement shows us is that we have to be very careful in our search for "hidden rules." It is possible for an intelligent explanation to torpedo a hidden rules argument, as John Bell so convincingly showed. We now know of two ways a possible supernatural explanation for phenomena can come to grief. The first is that the advance of science may discover rules governing apparently supernatural phenomena. One such example, of course, is the replacement of the theory that disease was caused by the displeasure of the gods with the germ theory of disease. The second is the ability to employ logic and mathematics, as did John Bell.

If you are a believer in supernatural phenomena, you might feel, as I do, that entanglement provides supporting evidence for the idea that I have put forth, that in an infinite Universe there must be regular phenomena which science will be unable to explain. My reason for this is simple. In a finite Universe, there is no such thing as an unexplainable phenomenon. In fact, the difficulty of explaining entanglement provides a smidgen of evidence that the Universe is not finite. That smidgen of evidence will disappear the moment somebody manages to explain entanglement, but it's at least one Nobel Prize away from happening.

Admittedly, you may not be convinced that the hidden variables hypothesis constitutes a potential supernatural phenomenon. You may feel this way for several possible reasons. One of the more likely reasons is that you haven't encountered the idea of entanglement before, and it doesn't really strike you as all that bizarre. Two photons emerge from an atom, they always spin the same direction—so what? It's much like the married couple you know that always have the same view; they've been married so long that it's not so surprising.

That's not the only thing that makes entanglement so surprising and a possible candidate for a supernatural phenomenon. It's that, prior to measuring one of the photons, neither photon has a defined spin direction. *Amazing though it may seem, the spin direction is not defined until you actually measure it!* It's similar to the idea that a marriage takes place between two people who have never met each other, and they amazingly think alike on every single issue, even though neither the husband nor the wife have ever even discussed any topics at all! This bizarre state of affairs—the fact that neither photon has a defined spin direction until it is measured—is a consequence of the Heisenberg Uncertainty Principle, of which you may have heard. One of the consequences of the Uncertainty Principle is that certain physical parameters are not precisely defined until the system in which they exist interacts with the outside world.

Schrodinger's Cat

The brilliant Austrian physicist Erwin Schrodinger, himself a Nobel Prize winner, gave an explanation of the Uncertainty Principle which has amused and perplexed since it was first propounded more than 75 years ago.[5] A box contains both a cat and a radioactive atom which has a precisely 50-percent chance of decaying (losing its radioactivity) in the next hour. If it should decay, it triggers a mechanism which breaks a vial of poisonous gas in the box; should that happen the cat will be killed (quickly and painlessly, for those readers who are cat-lovers). An hour passes. In what condition is the cat?

The obvious answer is that it's either alive or dead, and we'll know when we open the box. However, quantum mechanics says that until you check to see whether the atom has decayed or not, the atom is in a peculiar state. The state of the atom is not known precisely, but is a probability; it has decayed with a probability of 50 percent and has failed to decay with the same probability. The cat, therefore, has a 50-percent probability of being alive and a 50-percent probability of being dead. It's neither alive nor dead until we look.

Now, nobody has ever seen a cat that has a probability of 50 percent of being alive and a 50-percent probability of being dead. That's because the moment you see it, you know which it is. The same is true of the radioactive atom; the moment we see it we know whether it has decayed or not, but until we see it, we have no idea.

What makes this weird—but not supernatural, because it's a very well-understood phenomenon—is that we can make all sorts of accurate predictions using this description. In fact, lots of the wonderful electronic paraphernalia that exists today are constructed using our understanding of quantum mechanics. Moreover, this situation appears in the entanglement scenario we have been discussing, because the spins of the photons are not determined—*they do not even exist*—until they have been measured. The astounding thing, though, is that when the spins are measured around the same axis, thanks to entanglement, they always come out the same.

We can explain entanglement in the sense that we can predict the situations in which it occurs. We can also reject the hidden variables theory of entanglement which appears to be a very good candidate for a supernatural explanation of this phenomenon. Could there be other possible supernatural explanations? Maybe not for entanglement; we'll have to let the physicists sort that one out. That's why I said that there was a Nobel Prize waiting for you if you could come up with an alternative explanation to telepathy. Obviously, there is no way for photons to be in telepathic contact with each other, but they are in contact in some way, because they react identically.

Or are they? Remember, Albert Einstein referred to this as "spooky action at a distance." As yet, there is no explanation for this spooky action at a distance. Physicists call it *entanglement*, but just naming the phenomenon doesn't mean you understand it. Simply being able to produce really accurate measurements doesn't mean you understand something; it merely means you have developed a good "black box" for producing accurate measurements. It might, for instance, be possible to come up with diagnostic techniques for treating diseases effectively without ever understanding the germ theory of disease.

Supernatural Phenomena and Quantum Baloney

As you have probably realized by now, this chapter is not about telepathy but about quantum mechanics. That was a little sneaky, but if the chapter had been titled "Quantum Mechanics," or even "Quantum Mechanics and the Supernatural," I think there may have been a temptation on the part of some readers to skip the chapter, and I didn't want that.

One of the reasons that I didn't want that is because I have mentioned before that there's a tendency on the part of a lot of purveyors of the paranormal (and the sellers of the supernatural) to try to impress the potential customer by saying something along the lines of "Recent developments in quantum mechanics support this." Let's take a look at a few things that can be found on the Internet along these lines, and see if they stand up under analysis.

The brain's capabilities are the subject of a great deal of speculation, and this is where the possibility of the occurrence of supernatural phenomena enters the picture. The enormous reach of the Internet has enabled the question of supernatural powers of the human mind to be asked—and presumably answered—through the collective efforts of those connected to it. Here is an exchange from a few years back. The following question was asked of *Yahoo! Answers*: Does supernatural power in humans exist? Here is the best answer, as chosen by the Asker:

> Yes of course.
>
> Most, if not all humans use only 10 percent of their brain, mostly to talk, and do other physical, and mental things, but what is in the other 90%?
>
> Most can be used to actually talk to others through the mind, or even manipulate matter, and the dimensions.
>
> It is known in the Quantum Physics theory as well. We have a brain to do it, but not that opened door in our mind to do so.
>
> No matter what others say, one mind is the most powerful resource, thought, and weapon of all time. We all just have to open it.
>
> Manipulating matter means to like, move objects, heat, or cool things, shape items, or even create items. And dimensions, I mean like space, and time of course.
>
> It sounds fictional, but it isn't.[6]

Many people would undoubtedly concur with this answer. Let's take a close look at it. It is certainly true that humans generally use about 10 percent of their brain. However, when the person says that most (of the other 90 percent) can be used to actually talk to others through the mind, or even manipulate matter and the dimensions, he or she is claiming things that have not been established. Quantum physics has amazing revelations to its credit, but it says absolutely nothing about humans communicating with others telepathically. First of all, quantum physics has enough problems at the moment dealing with submicroscopic entities such as entangled photons. Quantum physics has a long way to go before it can say anything about such macroscopic entities as the human mind—if, indeed, it will ever be able to do so. The author of this particular statement is misusing quantum mechanics, asserting that it supports things it simply doesn't support, and is counting on the ignorance of his or her audience not to be able to detect the baloney.

One of the problems of writing seriously about the supernatural is that there's an awful lot of belief that is widely accepted for which there is absolutely no evidence. The person who asked the question blithely accepts the assertion that the human mind moves objects, heats and cools things, shapes and creates items, and does the same with space and time. This is unmitigated baloney, as the baloney detector will soon reveal.

Let's first look at moving an object. Here's the problem, at least from the standpoint of the scientist. In order to move an object, you need a force. This is Newton's First Law of Motion, which can be stated as follows: every object in a state of uniform motion tends to remain in that state unless acted upon by an external force. An object at rest is in a state of uniform motion; it's uniformly moving with zero velocity. So if the human mind can move objects, it is going to have to supply a force to do so.

Recall William Crookes' statement that new forces must be found to explain the work of the Universe. Possibly, just possibly, there exists a new force that science has not yet found, and the human mind can direct it. If so, this would be one of the most awesome discoveries in history—front page news on every newspaper, 24/7 coverage on radio and TV, and getting more hits on the Internet than anything else.

What about some of the other claims made in that response? Does the mind have the power to heat and cool things? Heating and cooling things runs headlong into the First Law of Thermodynamics: heat and work are forms of energy transfer. Shaping things requires work. Creating items collides with the Principle of Conservation of Mass-Energy; the total mass plus energy of a system remains the same, subject to Einstein's equation $E = mc^2$. Roughly speaking, mass and energy are the assets of the

Universe, and although they can be exchanged for one another, the total amount of assets remain the same.

There was at least one moment in the history of science when this principle was challenged. During the late 1940s, an alternative theory to the Big Bang was proposed called Continuous Creation. To explain the galaxies receding from each other, but keeping the long-term picture of the Universe the same (as it appeared to be at the time), Continuous Creation required the appearance of about one measly atom of hydrogen per cubic meter of space every billion years. Even so, that is absolutely radical from the standpoint of the Principle of Conservation of Mass-Energy, and my guess is that there were sighs of relief from many scientists when Continuous Creation was disproved.

Manipulating space and time is also well beyond any demonstrated power of the human mind. It is true that space and time are manipulated through the workings of the Universe. According to what we know about the Universe, space itself is expanding (I'll discuss this in a little more detail), and the rate at which time progresses changes as a function of both gravity and velocity (these are the General and Special Theories of Relativity, respectively). I'm willing to bet that if I were to confront the author of the Yahoo! Answers statement with the above information, I would be dismissed as one who has simply failed to open his mind. Scientists, I am sure he or she would say, don't have all the answers. And scientists would be the first ones to admit that, indeed, they don't have all the answers.

But the answers they do have seem to work awfully well, and no exception to their working has been found. The laws referred to earlier—Newton's Laws of Motion, the Laws of Thermodynamics, the Principle of Conservation of Mass-Energy—are as close as we have come to truth, other than the absolute truth which at the moment is obtainable only through mathematics and logic. Scientific laws are superseded—Newton's Law of Universal Gravitation was modified (slightly) in Einstein's Theory of General Relativity—but however minutely imperfect they may be, there are mountains of evidence on their side. In contrast, there is not a single scintilla of evidence of the existence of new forces or the ability of the mind to move objects, heat or cool things, etc.

There's a lot of similar material on the Internet. Here's a recent posting:

> There are various complicated and high level scientific theories that explain the power of the mind. Quantum physics is one of them. It explains that at the sub atomic level there is nothing but energy and that matter is nonexistent at that level. It also says that the presence of the energy is felt only because we observe it and thus shows us that the mind being the observer is actually a container of great power which needs to be harnessed for good use.
>
> Many scientists now believe that all so called 'supernatural' powers such as esp[sic], telepathy, remote viewing, psychic and clairvoyant phenomena can be explained in terms of quantum theory.
>
> In short—everything we see, hear and feel is merely a creation of our thoughts! Nothing is solid; it is all energy and this energy has been created by the power of our minds.[7]

Mmm, I don't think so. Brian Josephson notwithstanding, almost no reputable physicist believes that quantum physics explains the power of the mind, and I would guess that Josephson doesn't, either. Quantum physics does *not* say that at the subatomic level there is nothing but energy and that matter is nonexistent at that level. Matter and energy can be exchanged for one another according to Einstein's equation $E = mc^2$. We have performed experiments and made observations that show both of these to be true; we have seen energy exchanged for matter and matter for energy. However, dollars can be exchanged for gold and gold for dollars—but that doesn't mean that gold and dollars are the same thing. You can't make dollar fillings for your teeth.

Quantum physics does *not* say that the presence of energy is felt only because we observe it (this shows a complete lack of understanding of the Uncertainty Principle, but that's not surprising). Finally, it is most definitely not true that everything we see, hear, and feel has been created by the power of our minds. There is an objective Universe out there that has been around for 13.7 billion years. If the timespan of the life of the Universe is compressed to a single day, *homo sapiens* has been around for less than a second. Somebody will have to do a much better job than any Irving the Explainer to explain how something which has only been around for a few hundred thousand years can create a Universe which has been in existence for 14 billion years.

It's worth a look at the Website, which is currently offering an assortment of 30 items for about $16. The accompanying video is narrated by a gentleman with a British accent, which certainly helps make it more believable—but then, everything is more believable when presented with a British accent. Even though I am devoting this book to presenting what I believe to be a reasonable case for the existence of supernatural phenomena, there is no way that I can think of that I can tap into those phenomena.

Here's a final example from the baloney factory:

> Before you read further, I'd like to mention that the word "supernatural" may to some people seem to refer to something that goes against nature. Nothing could be further from truth. All abilities are developed in accord with natural laws. However, the natural laws do go beyond the world of Newtonian physics and move into the realm of quantum physics. These natural laws are laws of mind and spirit and these can and do over-ride the known laws of physics—as they relate to the physical dimension of experience.[8]

If the author had stopped before the last sentence, I'd have no problem with it. However, I'm willing to bet a significant amount of money that the author of those words cannot cite a single natural law of mind and spirit that can and does override the known laws of physics as they relate to the physical dimension of experience. I admit that the last sentence confuses me a little, and there's a loop-hole in it; I'd like to see the author's specific definition of "physical dimension of experience." Nonetheless, it sounds to me like the author is making a claim that laws of mind and spirit trump laws of physics. That's just not happening. The author can probably bag the $1,000,000 offered by James Randi to the first person to actually demonstrate paranormal abilities if they can show such a law of mind and spirit, and how it overrides the known laws of physics.

The brain is a truly remarkable organ, but it is an organ of this Universe and must function according to the known laws of physics. There is an 'out' here; physics is well aware that there are unknown laws which have not been discovered and which may never be discovered. However, as mentioned previously, the known laws work awfully well, and if there were an example of a natural law of mind and spirit which overrode the known laws of physics, those known laws of physics would not be laws.

Possibly I should cut the author of that last paragraph a little slack in the matter of "natural laws of mind and spirit." I don't doubt that there could be such laws; they might not be the type of laws with which the mathematical sciences deal, because they might not be capable of being expressed mathematically. One example of such a law might be "What goes around, comes around." To a certain extent, this is reminiscent of a law that can be expressed mathematically—Newton's Third Law of Motion, which states that to every action there is an equal and opposite reaction. "What goes around, comes around," is sometimes referred to as *karma*, but it is recognizable in other forms, such as "you reap what you sow."

This is not a law that is honored in every single instance; we all know of good people who keep getting unduly punished by circumstances. Conversely, there are individuals who appear to have few if any redeeming characteristics, yet somehow things always seem to work out for them. Nonetheless, I will cut the author zero slack with regard to the statement that they can and do override the known laws of physics.

Let me repeat that: absolutely nothing overrides the known laws of physics; that's why they are laws of physics. Duh. The brain is a truly remarkable organ, as I (and countless others) have stated before. But being of the Universe, it is subject to the laws of the Universe, especially the known laws of physics.

Let's put aside some of the nonsensical claims—nonsensical insofar as they have no experimental or measurable support—and turn to the remarkable things that have been documented that the brain is capable of doing. What is common to all those things that have been documented is that the brain is controlling internal—as opposed to external—reality. Yoga masters, for instance, have demonstrated the ability to enter trance-like states in which their breathing slows down considerably, and also can achieve a level of mastery over pleasure and pain. Many people have turned to yoga to increase their own capabilities of self-control, self-mastery, and self-realization—and this is possible because, after all, the brain is a controller analogous to the integrated chip that controls the functioning of an electronic device. Improve the controller and better control is possible—of the system that is being controlled, but not of the Universe.

10 Is the Universe Infinite?

If I had a way to establish whether the Universe were finite or infinite, I'd be booking my passage to Stockholm for my Nobel Prize. So you can safely assume that I don't have such a way, because the question on whether the Universe is finite or infinite has been a matter of scientific and non-scientific speculation for almost as long as we have been aware that there is a Universe.

Parallel Universes

There are different routes to a potentially infinite Universe, some involving quantum mechanics, and some not. However, one of the simplest possible ways to an infinite Universe is to have infinitely many close copies of our Universe. Most are different from our Universe, but it is possible to have identical copies. These copies, whether the same or different, are known as "parallel Universes."

The idea of parallel Universes is considerably older than the term "parallel Universe." Most of us have conjectured parallel Universes when we imagine how things would be different if we had made certain choices differently. My life changed considerably when my best friend in college and I decided to go to California for graduate school, rather than remain on the East Coast. Although the Beach Boys had yet to celebrate California girls, and although the Summer of Love was still a few years in the future, one thing was abundantly clear: the weather in California was a whole lot better than on the East Coast. The East Coast has snow in the winter, and hot and humid weather in the summer. So does Illinois, where my parents lived and where I returned when not at college. Besides, back in 1962, there was an allure to California which maybe, despite recent budgetary problems, it still possesses.

Going to California for grad school changed my life. I went to the University of California at Berkeley, and during the 1960s this was as good a place as any to be to witness the changes that were coming to American society. After that, I went to Los Angeles for my first teaching job, and have spent my life in Los Angeles ever since. I met my wife in Los Angeles, learned to play tennis and cultivate a healthy lifestyle in Los Angeles, and I am sure that I will spend most of the rest of my life here. Because my wife was born in Taiwan, I visited Asia—something I strongly doubt that I would have done had I married someone else, or not gotten married at all. All things considered, going to graduate school in California was a remarkably fortunate decision. But sometimes I wonder what would have happened if I'd remained on the East Coast for graduate school.

Of course, there's no way for me to know what would have happened, but certainly I would have a different circle of friends and there's no way that I would have married the same woman—our lives simply would not have intersected. I know that I'm fortunate, because many people who engage in the same sort of speculation do so on the basis of decisions they have made which have worked out badly—and mine worked out well.

This sort of thing makes for intriguing speculation, as well as intriguing fiction. The idea of a world—or a Universe—similar to our own in which things are slightly different, is a theme which has been pursued by science fiction writers in the past, as well as by television writers today. I first encountered this idea while in college, when I read Philip K. Dick's novel *The Man in the High Castle*, [1] a brilliantly entertaining novel describing a world in which the Axis powers had won World War II. The successful TV show *Fringe* (it's currently in its fourth season, which makes it successful by most standards), envisions an alternate Universe populated by many of the same characters as our own. In one Universe, a major character is a brilliant but ineffectual scientist, while in the alternate Universe he is a driven and influential politician.

The Man in the High Castle and *Fringe* are science fiction. But is something like this possibly science fact?

Science is an attempt to understand reality. It is certainly not the only such attempt, but I don't think there can be any question that it is the most successful. However, the discovery of quantum mechanics in the early portion of the 20th century raised puzzling questions about reality. At the everyday level, there is no question about what a table or an automobile is. It's a thing, with a definite location and a definite velocity: the table almost never moves and the car often does. As science probed the realm of the extremely small—the domain of atoms and electrons—quantum mechanics revealed that atoms and electrons were not "things" in the conventional sense. Unlike tables and automobiles, the Uncertainty Principle showed that an extremely small object could not be described by saying where it was and how fast it was moving. One could only say, for example, that it had a probability of being in a particular location. Electrons, formerly visualized as really tiny dots with negative electric charges, were described as "probability waves" in the mathematics of quantum mechanics—a mathematical description that has been shown to give experimental results which agree with predictions to at least 19 decimal places. To realize how extraordinary that is, we know that the Gross National Product of the United States is about 15 trillion dollars. Written out, that is $15,000,000,000,000.00. Accuracy to nineteen decimal places is analogous to knowing the Gross National Product of a world with 1,000 countries as wealthy as the United States—to the penny!

So how do you describe an object that is probably not what we think of as an object at all? Werner Heisenberg, the discoverer of the Uncertainty Principle, struggled with this as well. In attempting to describe the quantum theory, Heisenberg stated that "In the experiments about atomic events we have to do with things and facts, with phenomena that are just as real as any phenomena in daily life. But the atoms or the elementary particles themselves are not as real; they form a world of potentialities or possibilities rather than one of things or facts."[2]

The first physicists to truly come to grips with quantum mechanics were every bit as perplexed as Heisenberg when attempting to understand what quantum mechanics said about the nature of reality. A famous quote by Niels Bohr is that "If quantum mechanics hasn't profoundly shocked you, then you haven't understood it yet."[3] Niels Bohr was Danish, and was one of the physicists who produced a view of quantum mechanics that came to be known as the Copenhagen Interpretation. The Copenhagen Interpretation of quantum mechanics, to which many physicists both past and present subscribe, essentially sweeps the problem of describing reality under the rug. It says that quantum mechanics is merely a method of computing the probabilities of certain variables which can neither be described as particles (macroscopic objects) or waves, such as electromagnetic vibrations.

No one can deny the effectiveness of quantum mechanics as a practical tool; most of the high-tech electronic gadgetry we enjoy today, from computers to magnetic resonance imagers, relies on computations based on the theory. However, it's very unsatisfactory to have a theory which we cannot interpret; it's somewhat similar to having an oracle deliver pronouncements from on high. Even though we can rely on what the oracle tells us—and, indeed, we developed this particular oracle—it would be nice to know what's going on underneath the surface.

Unfortunately, we still don't know for sure what the underlying nature of reality is. The Copenhagen Interpretation begs the question—but in the late 1950s a graduate student came up with an explanation of reality that is consistent with quantum mechanics. This explanation is as bizarre as many of the more arcane theories from science fiction; indeed, it actually is one of the more arcane theories of science fiction. Despite that, it is accepted by many scientists as the most consistent view of quantum mechanics that actually coincides with reality.

The theory, later to become known as the Many-Worlds Interpretation of quantum mechanics, was the key idea of the doctoral dissertation of Hugh Everett, a brilliant student at Princeton University, whose thesis advisor was John Archibald Wheeler. Briefly stated, the Many-Worlds Interpretation of quantum mechanics declares that all possible alternative histories and futures are real, and result in actual realities. We know, for instance, that when a fair coin is flipped, it has a 50-percent probability of coming up heads and a 50-percent probability of coming up tails. The Many-Worlds Interpretation is that both things happen—a lot. Roughly speaking, when the coin is flipped, the Universe splits into two different Universes. In one, the coin lands heads, and in the other, it lands tails.

This generates a lot of Universes—hence the term *Many-Worlds.* For example, let's suppose that at the same time that the coin is being flipped, an atom is possibly decaying, and a young lady is deciding whether to accept the invitation of a young man to go out on a date. Each of these events has two different alternatives, and there are Universes in which all eight possible combinations of these events occur. I won't list all eight here, but one possible Universe has the coin coming up heads, the atom decaying, and the young lady deciding to go out on the date. However, the key feature of Everett's construction is that if one looks at all possible Universes, in 50 percent of them the coin came up heads, and in 50 percent of them the coin came up tails. Possibly the young lady was three times as likely to accept the invitation as not—that would correspond to a 75-percent probability that she would accept the invitation. So in 75 percent of the Universes she would accept the date, and in 25 percent of them she would not.

Although it is known as the Many-Worlds Interpretation of quantum mechanics, it obviously fits neatly into the framework of parallel Universes. There is also something very satisfying about it—if you had dreams of pursuing a career as a rock star but decided to go into business because it was more secure, the Many-Worlds Interpretation says that somewhere not only did you become a rock star, but you became a legend. Of course, there are also those Universes where your career as a rock star flamed out, you had no back-up plan, and you are waiting on tables in some greasy diner.

What we really want to know, though, from the standpoint of this book, is whether the possibility of parallel Universes would allow supernatural or paranormal phenomena to occur in our Universe. In order to come up with an answer to that question, let's take a look at a systematic treatment of parallel Universes.

Perhaps the most complete study of this subject that is accessible to a general audience can be found in a tremendously thought-provoking article in the May 2003 issue of *Scientific American.* In "Parallel Universes,"[4] Max Tegmark presents a taxonomy of different variations of the parallel Universe idea. His article starts off as follows:

Tegmark starts his article by asking if there is an identical copy of you somewhere else in the Universe, who resides on another Earth in the same city that you live. The only difference between the life of your alter ego and you occurs after you read the first paragraph of the article. You decide to continue reading, but your alter ego puts down the article to do something else.

He goes on to mention that, no matter how utterly bizarre it may seem that there is an identical copy of you who has lived an identical life to yours on a planet that looks exactly like Earth, it is a consequence of the simple assumption that space is infinite and uniformly filled with matter. This assumption is held by a number of cosmologists, and agrees with current astronomical observations.

This is an extremely intriguing article, and it contains material which, in conjunction with the points made in this book, opens the door to supernatural phenomena—phenomena which are a part of the real world, but which cannot be explained by science. Let's take a look at Tegmark's classification of the different types of parallel Universes.

The Level I Universes consists of those Universes which are "out there" but simply cannot be seen because of the speed of light limitation. Those Universes would exist in a model of physics which incorporates something called "chaotic inflation." It isn't necessary to know what "chaotic inflation" is—at least for our purposes—but the important thing is that space would go on forever. That might be a bad way of phrasing it, because the word forever is generally thought to refer to time, but there would be no end to space. Our particular segment of this Universe consists of all points from which we can receive information; the Big Bang currently sets the maximum distance from which we can receive information to about 13.7 billion light-years. Assuming that 1) the Universe is infinite, 2) mass is reasonably uniformly distributed across the entire Universe, and 3) the laws of physics and chemistry that hold in our chunk of the Universe apply everywhere else, it follows that not only must there be another chunk of the Universe that looks like ours; there must be infinitely many such chunks. It's the tic-tac-toe problem all over again; there are only so many ways of arranging the pieces, and if you have infinitely many tic-tac-toe games, there will be a lot of repetitions. Assuming that the tic-tac-toe games are played without bias—so that you don't have a situation in which all tic-tac-toe games start with an X in the center, or something like that—there will be infinitely many copies of all possible tic-tac-toe games.

This is one of the cornerstones that led to my acceptance of the idea that supernatural phenomena could become part of a scientific view of the Universe. The other, equally important, piece of the puzzle was the application of Godel's Incompleteness Theorem to a model of the Universe in which the Peano Axioms for the integers hold. In a Universe satisfying (1) and (2), we have the Peano Axioms applying to both mass and length, two of the fundamental physical parameters on which scientific theories are based. In such a Universe, there must be mathematical relations satisfied by mass and length which can *never* be proved by logic. To me, this means that there are principles that mass and length obey, but which science—ours or anyone else's—can never deduce. There would be physical theories that we might guess or surmise, but never prove.

This is all we need in the way of parallel Universes to incorporate supernatural phenomena, but there is a reasonable caveat to be offered. The basic parameters of physical theories are mass, length, and time. However, chaotic inflation theories are a sub-class of what are termed "eternal inflation" theories. And, yes, "eternal inflation" is just that; it goes on forever. Tegmark's Level I Universes are thus a natural home for supernatural phenomena as they are defined here. And, according to Tegmark, it agrees with all the evidence we have so far.

It is instructive as well as entertaining to look at the remaining three levels in Tegmark's classification of parallel Universes. Level II Universes look sort of like Level I Universes, except that the physical constants such as the speed of light and absolute zero might differ from Universe to Universe. In some Universes, light might travel much more slowly or much more quickly, and absolute zero might be a lot colder or a lot warmer. The view of the Multiverse (the all-encompassing entity that contains all these parallel Universes) is that space is continually stretching, but in some places the stretching stops and a Universe is created—much like a bubble in a bowl of soup. Each of these bubbles forms a Level I Universe, so if this is the correct picture, supernatural phenomena occur in Level II Universes as well.

The Level III Universes are the ones that occur if Everett's Many-Worlds Interpretation of quantum mechanics holds. There is a qualitative difference between Level I Universes and Level III Universes. We can understand the difference by using Tegmark's example of the reader of the article who decides to continue reading in one Universe but puts it aside in another. In the Many-Worlds Interpretation, the two Universes diverge and do not interact with each other. If the probability is three out of four that the reader continues to read—and why shouldn't he or she, as it's a very interesting article—in three out of every four of the Universes, the reader continues, but the Universes are separate entities. One can think of a tree branching out with the following restriction: once one has gone on along one branch, it is no longer possible to go onto another branch. In a Level I Universe, there is simply an infinite amount of space, and three of every four Universes similar to ours contain readers who are continuing. An analogy would be an infinite checkerboard in which three of every four squares are red. Contact with another version of yourself might be possible in a Level I Universe—providing such minor details as traveling faster than light are ironed out (this is typical of the humor one finds at a scientific conference)—but the twain can never meet in a Level III Universe, for they are on paths that can never contact each other.

Tegmark also postulates Level IV Universes, which are all possible examples of things that can be described as mathematical structures. I must say that here Tegmark loses me. Although I believe that mathematics has an incredible diversity of structures, I don't believe that all of them are qualified to be Universes. For instance, mathematics describes sets with specific numbers of objects in them—the set of the days of the week, for instance, is a set with precisely 7 elements in it. There are many other things that can be described as a set with 7 elements in it, such as the number of points awarded in football for scoring a touchdown and kicking the extra point, but I find it hard to believe that somewhere there is a real Universe with precisely 7 things in it—no more, no less. And this says nothing about some of the bizarre structures that mathematics examines. When I was working during graduate school, a picture circulated of an object described as a Mark IV blivet—although you've probably never seen one, here's an image for you to peruse.

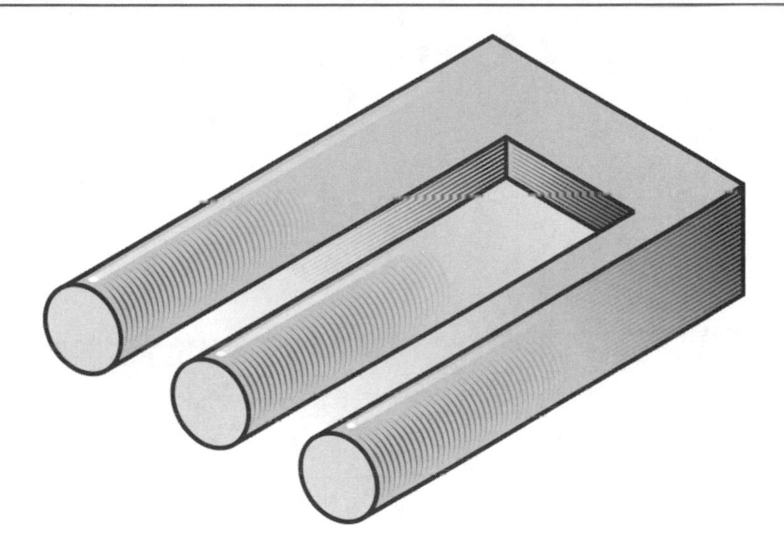

When you look at it, you will realize that the object "pictured" cannot exist in the real world. There are numerous such objects in mathematics which cannot be placed in our three-dimensional Universe, although it is possible to describe higher-dimensional Universes in which such objects would make sense. However, mathematics is not only infinite, it is more infinite than you or I—or Tegmark—can possibly imagine. This level of infinity is more than enough for supernatural phenomena to exist, but it's sort of like saying how many angels can dance on the head of a pin. Supernatural phenomena might exist in abundance in such a Universe, but it's not a Universe to which we can relate, and so I consider supernatural phenomena in this context to be basically irrelevant to the type of phenomena I describe in this book.

Summing it up, though, there is plenty of room for the infinite in the parallel Universes that could be sensibly accepted by many scientists. If there's room for the infinite, as I have asserted, there should be plenty of room for supernatural or paranormal phenomena.

11 The Paranormal Through the 20th Century

It's time to examine the past, present, and future of the paranormal; at least that portion of what are referred to as paranormal phenomena that I feel that science and mathematics can comfortably investigate. This leaves out the weird stuff.

So what's left? After some thought, I've narrowed it down to five different categories: ESP, telepathy, remote viewing, psychokinesis, and precognition. My opinion is that the science with which I am familiar has something to say about each one of these. I'll look at each one of these by presenting a case from the record that is typically cited as supporting each as a genuine example of paranormal phenomena. After that I'll look at how science either did look or would have looked at it prior to the turn of the millennium.

I'm choosing the turn of the millennium for a particular reason that has nothing to do with Y2K, harmonic convergence, or anything like that. The Universe we know began to change significantly with the new millennium. The Universe itself did not change, of course, but our view of it did, and in some cases the new view may have an impact. I think we've learned some things in the last decade or so which may have a bearing on the phenomena under discussion, and I'll use the last chapter to call attention to these.

For the record, I'm not counting this book under the heading of "new view with impact." As I've mentioned, I don't believe I've made a serious error that would invalidate the position I've expounded here, and I hope that sometime in the future, this book does come under the heading of "new view with impact." Time will tell.

ESP (Extra-Sensory Perception)

Without a doubt, the most extensive series of tests on ESP were performed over decades by Professor Joseph Banks Rhine of Duke University.[1] Rhine began his career as a botanist, but switched to parapsychology shortly afterwards. If parapsychology is to be classified as a science, it is largely because of the efforts of Rhine, who devoted decades to the research. Rhine founded both the *Journal of Parapsychology* and the Parapsychological Association.

One of Rhine's early subjects who seemingly possessed parapsychological abilities was Adam Linzmayer, a Duke economics major. Rhine performed a series of Zener-card tests on Linzmayer. Anyone who watches paranormal shows on TV or in the movies has undoubtedly seen Zener cards, which have symbols such as circles, stars, and wavy lines. Linzmayer initially had extraordinary scores, far in excess of what would have been expected by chance. Over time, however, Linzmayer's scores declined significantly, to slightly above what would have been expected by chance.

This scenario was to be repeated with some frequency in Rhine's lab. A test subject would initially obtain results far in excess of chance results, but after a while the scores would return to chance or near-chance success rates. This decline was sometimes attributed to boredom or distraction on the part of the subject. We can understand that this might have been the case; many skills, such as the ability to play a game or a musical instrument, decline if boredom or distraction enters the picture. This explains why the fundamental injunction in practically all games is "Watch the ball!"

The noted author Martin Gardner, one of the members of the Committee for the Skeptical Inquiry, made numerous criticisms of Rhine's methodology. To Rhine's credit, he wrote a paper in which he reported some of the fraud associated with his investigations. Gardner points out that no one else has been able to duplicate Rhine's positive results. Duplication of results is one of the key points on which scientific acceptance is based.

The track record displayed by Linzmayer and other test subjects—initial strong results which gradually fade with time—can also be accounted for by a statistical phenomenon known as *regression to the mean.*

We've all had days where everything goes right. If you're a golfer, all your drives land in the fairway, and you sink all the short putts and a bunch of long putts. If you drive to work, there are those days where everything goes smoothly and you hit all the lights just as they change from red to green.

Conversely, we've all had days where nothing goes right. For the golfer, the drives always seem to find the rough, the iron shots find the sand traps, and all the putts lip out. When you're driving to work, all the lights change from green to red just as you get close to the intersection.

These days, as we know, are atypical. If you're a golfer, most of your days on the course are average: some shots are good, some shots are bad, in accordance with your handicap. When you drive to work, some lights are green, some lights are red—and most of the time, the time it takes you to get to work is about the same.

The idea of regression to the mean is that over a long period of time, exceptionally unusual results will tend to become less and less frequent, and your results will return, or regress, to the mean result (mean is another word for average). If you're a golfer, your good games (and bad ones) will generally be followed by roughly average games, because that's the golfer that you are. Your daily scores will tend towards your mean score, because that's who you are as a golfer. If you're a driver, the days that you make exceptionally good time or exceptionally bad time will generally tend towards your mean driving time, because that's what your driving time usually is.

Results such as those obtained by Rhine in the case of Adam Linzmayer and others can be explained by regression to the mean. An individual will initially achieve remarkable success—but over a period of time that success will fade away.

Telepathy

Telepathy is the extrasensory perception of another person's thoughts. To some extent, this subsumes the experiments described in the previous section, but it more often refers to the sensing of what another person is experiencing. These often seem related to the emotional intensity of the experience, as there are many stories of spouses sensing when their partners are experiencing danger, and of course there are similar stories involving parents sensing similar situations involving their children.

There are accounts that telepathy has been achieved, and in some cultures, it is viewed as a routine human capability. Taylor gives descriptions of several accounts of telepathy among the Balinese, with the veracity of this assertion attested to by an American woman, Mrs. K.E. Mershon, who lived on Bali from 1931 to 1941. She wrote that ESP was part of the everyday life of the Balinese people, and that if someone wanted to get you to come to their house, they would "call you on the wind"—summon you by sending a mental message. Mrs. Mershon relates a story where she visited a village, only to find that the people there were annoyed with her because she had not come earlier. They insisted that they had sent for her the previous day by sending a mental message. Mrs. Mershon asserts that calling on the wind was a standard method of communication in Bali, and that she herself had acquired proficiency at it. According to Taylor, a Cornell professor who had lived on Bali for many years, stated that "They believe these powers are partly a natural gift but that they can be partly accentuated by meditation and spiritual discipline."[2] These powers, however, seem to atrophy when the culture is brought up to speed by acquiring technology, such as telephone and radio, which reduces the need for the ability of calling on the wind.

The letter psi is the 23rd letter of the Greek alphabet. It's frequently used in quantum mechanics to denote a wave function, but it is also used as an abbreviation for various paranormal faculties, possibly because it is pronounced very similarly to the first syllable of "psychic."

Martin Gardner, in an article entitled *Parapsychology and Quantum Mechanics*, states that "Parapsychologists differ considerably about the 'facts' of their trade, but there is a fairly solid core of beliefs on which most of them agree. They are convinced that psi powers (ESP and PK) are possessed in some degree by everybody, and to a high degree by a few. Almost all agree that psi forces are independent of time and distance."[3]

A telepathic experiment was conducted by astronaut Edgar Mitchell during the 1971 flight of Apollo 14, in conjunction with several participants on Earth.[4] Mitchell concentrated on sending random number sequences; two of the people who were stationed on Earth did somewhat better than chance in correctly identifying the sequences. This is sometimes cited as evidence that the telepathic ability does not diminish with distance. You may recall that one of the problems Einstein had with telepathy as a manifestation of a psi force was that all the known forces do diminish with distance.

If psi forces are independent of distance, then, as Crookes says, new forces will definitely have to be found to do the work of the Universe, because the four forces that we know are most definitely dependent upon distance. Gravitation and electromagnetism fall off as the square of the distance; if the distance between two masses (or electric charges) is tripled (for instance, changing the distance between them from 2 feet to 6 feet), the strength of the forces falls off by a factor of $9 = 3^2$. The weak force, which is responsible for radioactive decay, is limited to extremely short distances, considerably less than a quadrillionth of an inch. The strong force is likewise constrained, operating only within atomic dimensions. If psi forces are actually forces, they are none of the forces we have observed.

Remote Viewing

Clairvoyance is the supposed ability to see objects or events not directly perceived by the senses. Remote viewing, as described earlier in the book, is a type of clairvoyance. This is one of the most thoroughly tested types of paranormal abilities. Indeed, as Taylor remarks, "If clairvoyance truly does occur, then it should ultimately be possible to capture it in the laboratory."[5] The tests by J. B. Rhine at Duke tested one type of clairvoyance. Another test, which was mentioned earlier in the book as an experiment which was published in the prestigious journal *Nature*, was conducted by Puthoff and Targ at the Stanford Research Institute in California in the 1970s. Subjects were tested on their ability to describe target locations while they were being visited by a member of the investigative team. The team member would drive to a location and describe it, the subjects would attempt to come up with descriptions paralleling those of the investigative team. One of the subjects, a former California police commissioner, definitely seemed to be able to receive information with a considerable degree of accuracy; in one case he actually named the location to which the team member had driven. However, David Marks looked into the transcripts of the reports, and discovered that sensory cues and editing had taken place but not been mentioned.

As I mentioned earlier, my friend Linda was invited to a seminar on remote viewing conducted by an individual who presumably was connected with a military program to locate Saddam Hussein using that technique. The military has spent considerable sums over the years on research related to psychic abilities, especially when it learned during the Cold War that the Chinese and the Russians had projects in this area. These projects were known collectively as the Stargate Project.[6] Although there were claims that some of the viewers had successfully described a new type of Soviet strategic submarine and also located a downed Russian bomber in Africa, the military eventually scrapped the program on the grounds that no useful information had ever been shown to come as a result. It was also discovered that project managers had altered reports to fit in with intelligence from other areas.

In 2001 and 2002, the United Kingdom performed a study on 18 untrained subjects. The E and H fields (which are vector fields associated with electricity and magnetism respectively) were measured in the vicinity of the subjects in an attempt to find correlations between changes in these fields and successful remote viewing experiences. There was no evidence that the subjects had successful remote viewing experiences, and the project was terminated.[7]

Part of the difficulty in establishing creditable results for the phenomenon of remote viewing is that in order to be scientifically valid, results must be replicable. This has never been accomplished. Although the claim could be made that remote viewing is a skill that only certain individuals possess, the James Randi Institute has offered a $1,000,000 prize to anyone successfully demonstrating this ability. According to the Institute, none of the applicants for the prize has even passed the preliminary tests.

Precognition

I'm going to spend more time on precognition because it is the paranormal phenomenon with which most people have had some experience, either directly or secondhand. For instance, almost every major disaster brings reports of people who claim to have had a premonition of it. Even animals are often cited as being able to sense future disasters. As a Californian, my experience is that almost every major earthquake will bring calls into talk radio saying something like "My dog went crazy; that only happens before an earthquake."

We have spent some time discussing the forces in the Universe, from the standpoint of physics, but in order to understand precognition, it is necessary to understand the structure of the Universe as physics sees it. Although there are some theories which hypothesize an 11-dimensional Universe, the most widely accepted theory is that the Universe is a four-dimensional structure; three spatial dimensions (up-down, left-right, and forward-backward) and one time dimension. Time is different from the other dimensions in that we can only move in a single direction in the time dimension. Spatially, we can move forward or backward, left or right, up or down—but we can only move forward in time. Explanations of this have not been easy to come by—and although we can travel forward in time at faster rates (we know this as a consequence of Einstein's Theory of Relativity, and it has been experimentally demonstrated), we have yet to find an explanation as to why we cannot travel backward in time. Indeed, although we are fairly certain that we cannot do so, we haven't been able to prove conclusively that it is impossible—and certainly, no one has actually traveled back in time.

The Universe as Western science sees it is a four-dimensional structure in which matter resides and is acted upon by the various forces. Western science sees the Universe (or at least the portion of it that we can see and have seen) from inside. We are embedded in that four-dimensional structure. But this raises two questions; one that math and science are willing to tackle, and one that they are not. The question that math and science are comfortable confronting is whether it is possible to see a Universe from outside. There is a wonderful book called *Flatland*,[8] written in 1884, by the English school teacher Edwin Abbott Abbott (no, that's not a misprint, his middle name really was the same as his last name). *Flatland* describes a Universe, and its inhabitants, which is confined to two spatial dimensions. *Flatland* is a really intriguing book for several reasons. Literary critics probably think of it as a satire on the Victorian era, much as Jonathan Swift's better-known *Gulliver's Travels* was a satire on the world of Swift's time.

Abbott wrote his books under the pseudonym "A Square." In the two-dimensional world Flatland, of which A Square is an inhabitant, women are simple line segments, while men are polygons with varying numbers of sides (A Square, of course, has four). A Square is a member of a social caste of four-sided figures, who dreams of a visit to Lineland, a one-dimensional line, and finds it impossible to convince the monarch of that realm of the existence of two-dimensional figures. The same thing happens when Flatland is visited by a sphere; the residents of Flatland have difficulty comprehending Spaceland, the land of three dimensions.

I'm not sure how effective *Flatland* was as satire (you can read it and decide for yourself), but of course it is fascinating from the standpoint of describing the peculiarities of worlds of varying dimensions. From our standpoint, what is important is that A Square sees Lineland from outside. Abbott has pointed out that it is possible for a creature to observe a Universe from outside, which may not seem as surprising now as it was then. A Square recognizes that the inhabitants of Lineland are unable to conceive of higher dimensions, and the inhabitants of Flatland have similar problems visualizing spatial objects.

Mathematics has no difficulty visualizing objects of higher dimension than three or four; in fact, in some ways the mathematics of infinite-dimensional spaces is easier than the mathematics of finite-dimensional ones. We can *imagine* multi-dimensional Universes from inside, but can we view our own Universe, as it were, from outside? That's the second question, and math and science generally do not go there, although Einstein may have perceived the Universe as an object which could conceivably be viewed from the outside. Although Einstein did not explicitly state it this way, he did remark that "The distinction between past, present, and future is only an illusion, even if a stubborn one."[9]

However, other disciplines—and other cultures—are more willing to venture in this direction. In his poem *I See the Four-fold Man*,[10] William Blake writes, "I see the Past, Present, and Future existing all at once, Before me." This is an amazing poem, considering that the Universe viewed as a mathematical object is called a four-dimensional manifold by differential geometers. Blake also rings in the discoverer of the Theory of Universal Gravitation in the same poem, when he says:

> For Bacon and Newton, sheath'd in dismal steel, their terrors hang
>
> Like iron scourges over Albion: reasonings like vast serpents
>
> Infold around my limbs, bruising my minute articulations.

Now I don't think for a minute that Blake has foretold that Einstein's theory of four-dimensional space-time would supersede Newton's Theory of Universal Gravitation. Precognition, the knowledge of events that are yet to come, would certainly fall under the heading of a paranormal occurrence, yet such knowledge would be routine for an outsider who could view the entirety of our four-dimensional spacetime. Past, present, and future would indeed exist for such an outsider, who would be both outside space and outside time.

The problem with viewing the Universe from outside is that, if we could see into the future, we would violate causality, the principle that causes must precede effects. Suppose that our Universe is embedded in some larger structure, much as Abbott's two-dimensional Flatland could be regarded as a plane in a three-dimensional space. Suppose also that it was possible in some way to obtain information about the entire Universe, its past, present, and future. That's what precognition purports to be: there is information available about the future, and it can be obtained.

To some extent, physics does that already. The orbits of astronomical bodies are, to a large extent, predictable. Let's say that we discover a meteor which will impact the Earth at some time in the future. We have obtained information about the future! Now, we use that information to change the course of the future by either destroying the meteor or changing its course slightly so that it does not impact the Earth. Haven't we changed the future? Of course not, because that future hasn't happened yet, we have used our knowledge to extrapolate what will happen in the future, as unequivocally determined by what we can observe in the present. I do this every year just before my anniversary, because I can just imagine the carnage if I fail to appropriately commemorate this memorable event. I use my knowledge to extrapolate what will happen in the future in order to avoid the potentially disastrous impact from the 'marital meteor' that will result if I forget our anniversary.

How does this differ from, say, obtaining information that if I take a certain route home, I will suffer serious injury from a traffic accident, and thus take a different route home? The obvious difference is that, in the case of the meteor impact, knowledge is obtained about what will happen in the future as unequivocally determined by what can be observed in the present. If I can obtain information about the impending traffic accident by using what I know about the present, there is no logical inconsistency. If, however, I obtain this information via some sort of message from a future which has not yet happened, by avoiding the accident I invalidate the message, and therefore I could not have been sent the message that the accident would happen, because it didn't!

This raises all sorts of logical problems. First of all, it makes me doubt the validity of any message I think I receive from the future, because if I can take actions based on that message, I can invalidate the accuracy of that message. So let's try changing what the message says. Instead of saying, "You will be injured in a traffic accident on the San Diego Freeway tomorrow night," it says, "If you drive on the San Diego Freeway tomorrow night, you will be injured in a traffic accident." We have changed the content of the message from a definitive prediction to a hypothetical one. Do we run into logical inconsistencies this way?

Let's see. If we avoid the San Diego Freeway, we have not invalidated the message, but we have rendered it trivially true. Any "if... then" statement with a false premise is trivially true; the message might just as well have said, "If New York City is in the state of California, then you will be injured in a traffic accident." If we take the San Diego Freeway and are injured in a traffic accident, then the message was correct—but so what? For all we know, this identical message was sent to a million different drivers in Southern California. For some of them it will be true; for most, fortunately it will be false. Finally, if we take the San Diego Freeway and are not injured, the message is false—which will probably make us less likely to believe in apparent messages from the future.

Precognition is ruled out by physics on the basis of logical inconsistencies such as the one described above—yet there are thousands of examples of precognition in which people accurately predicted the future. How are these two ideas compatible? The link comes from statistics, and I alluded to it in the previous paragraph.

It is quite likely that you, or someone you know, awakened in the middle of the night with the sense that something has happened to a loved one. A phone call was then made to find out if everything was all right, with the result that there was nothing wrong and there was no cause for alarm. I know this has happened to me, and I'm sure it has happened to countless others. No one pays attention, and these results are never reported.

The dull, the mundane, and the uninteresting are just as much a part of the data that should be collected as the out-of-the-ordinary, the fascinating, and the interesting. But, quite often, they never are. As a result, we do not have the complete picture. Although there is no way to substantiate this, since the relevant data is never collected, I'm sure that if all our "precognitions" were tabulated, a few would be right, the vast majority would be wrong—and that's what we could expect from statistics. We could even expect that there would be a few people among the billions on Earth who would have eye-popping percentages of correct predictions. These people might be labeled by some as seers. But if everyone on Earth flipped a coin 25 times, we could expect that more than 100 would flip 25 consecutive heads. Large data sets contain individual events that look improbable when considered separately.

Psychokinesis

Because this book is deliberately avoiding the weird stuff, I'm avoiding possible sources of psychokinetic activity, such as poltergeists. I've already discussed psychokinetic hoaxes such as Uri Geller's alleged ability to start watches by power of thought. There are other presumed examples of psychokinetic phenomena which, on closer examination, have been shown to be the result of electrostatic phenomena. One such case, reported by Taylor, involved a woman named Alla Vinogradova, who could reportedly move aluminum cigar tubes (these are very lightweight) and other lightweight objects by making pushing motions at them from a distance.[11] Although no fraud was taking place here, videotapes revealed that Vinogradova was rubbing her hands together prior to the experiment, and this is known to generate a strong electrostatic field. Anyone who has rubbed their hand across their hair on a cold day and then touched a doorknob can attest to this.

It's worth noting that there have been some extremely mysterious effects that it has taken scientists some time to unravel, and which have occasionally been attributed to an incorrect cause. One of my favorite such instances occurred in 1967, when Jocelyn Bell Burnett and Anthony Hewish discovered a source emitting pulses at 1.33 second intervals by using a radio telescope.[12] A number of possible explanations, both terrestrial and extraterrestrial, were eliminated. Although Bell (she was unmarried at the time) and Hewish did not actually believe that they had found a lighthouse operated by aliens, they nonetheless gave the source the tentative name LGM-1; LGM being an acronym for Little Green Men. After several other such sources were discovered, the Little Green Men hypothesis was abandoned in favor of a pulsating neutron star, now known as a pulsar.

In presumed cases of psychokinesis, one thing should always be remembered: the classical physical principle of Conservation of Energy (updated by the Theory of Relativity to the Principle of Conservation of Mass-Energy) is not just a good idea; it's the law. According to work done by the American mathematician Emmy Noether, the principle of Conservation of Energy is a consequence of the fact that the laws of physics do not change over time.[13] Psychokinesis violates the Conservation of Energy, and that unequivocally rules it out.

• • • • • • • • • • • • • • •

At the turn of the millennium, things were looking pretty bleak for the five paranormal phenomena we have discussed here. Well-established physics had completely invalidated both precognition and psychokinesis. ESP, telepathy, and remote viewing could best be described by being on life support.

But things change.

12 The Changing Universe and the Future of Paranormality

There was an excellent series on television a number of years ago entitled *The Day the Universe Changed.* The series was hosted by James Burke, author of the fascinating book *Connections,*[1] and described pivotal events which altered our view of the Universe.

The Universe that we see today is very different from the Universe we saw a few years before Y2K. Most of these changes are the result of scientific advances. Even as I write this book, I read of developments which may have an impact on some of the phenomena I have discussed.

However, I don't want to write this chapter and leave the impression that I believe the Universe is a mystical place, with the new developments in science substituting for quantum mechanics as the justification for what the purveyors of the paranormal are presently pushing. So let me make my position clear from the outset.

Overall, I have roughly the same point of view as Lord Rayleigh, the Nobel Prize–winner and former president of the Society for Psychical Research. I recognize that the research that has been done from a scientific standpoint has shown no evidence of the existence of any paranormal phenomena that is replicable in a laboratory, but there are more than enough unexplained incidents to justify continuing efforts to investigate them. I think science does itself a disservice in saying "absolutely not," rather than saying "no evidence yet, but not closing the books." Not only can science not say "absolutely not" with complete assurance, but encouraging open-minded investigation is critical to science. There are too many cases in the past where the prevailing scientific paradigm has been shown to be completely wrong.

I believe, as do a number of scientists, that the Universe is infinite. I am convinced that there is an axiomatic structure for physics (as yet this has not been established; it was one of the famous 23 problems that David Hilbert set for the mathematical community in 1900) which must incorporate the Peano Axioms for the integers. As a result, I believe there are true propositions expressing relationships between the measurable quantities of physics which can never be proved. I see no reason not to refer to these relationships as supernatural, because they transcend science—not just science as we know it, but science as we can ever know it. I strongly suspect that most of those relationships will never be relevant to our lives, but some might, and maybe some already are.

I also believe, as do some of the logicians with whom I have talked, that almost all propositions dealing with the measurable quantities of physics are unknowable in the sense described in the previous paragraph. I believe that at some stage logicians of the future will be able to describe "almost all" more exactly, just as mathematicians have an exact description for the statement that "almost all" real numbers are irrational.

Finally, I believe that many scientists of the past and present hold views similar to this, in the sense of Newton's "great ocean of undiscovered truth." The only real question is whether the great ocean consists of truths that we will simply not be able to discover because humanity's time and resources are limited, or because those truths are unknowable to any entities that may pursue such knowledge.

Although not the latest word on the subject, a 1994 survey of 1,100 college professors in the United States found that 55 percent of natural scientists, 66 percent of social scientists outside of psychology, and 77 percent of the remainder (mostly liberal arts and education) believe that ESP is either an established fact or a likely possibility.[2] Only 34 percent of psychologists held this belief, possibly because they come across more people who believe in ESP but are clearly dysfunctional in some way. Even so, I find these numbers extremely impressive. These are highly educated people, and my guess is that a similar survey conducted on the entire population would find higher numbers. I would expect the natural scientists to be familiar with Newton's enunciation of the "great ocean of undiscovered truth," and I think that many of those who believe in ESP or other paranormal phenomena have reached a similar conclusion for roughly the same reason. There's just way too much that is not yet known, and we're only beginning to get a handle on how wide and deep the great ocean is.

The Dark Side

It is not only the duty, but the passion, of scientists to investigate new phenomena. It is only in the last 40 years or so that we have discovered that the portion of the Universe for which we have an adequate description comprises less than 5 percent of the Universe, giving scientists a whole new class of phenomena to investigate.

Vera Rubin is an American astronomer who pointed out the first serious discrepancy between our description of the Universe and the way the Universe actually is. She was studying the rotation rates of stars around the center of the galaxy to which they belong. Rotation rates of celestial objects have been studied for centuries; in fact, they are the subject of Kepler's Laws. One of Kepler's Laws can be used to determine the rotation rates of the planets around the Sun: the farther away from the Sun that a planet is, the longer it takes to rotate around the Sun. Mercury is the closest planet to the Sun; it takes 88 days for it to complete a single revolution. The Earth, of course, takes one year to revolve around the Sun and Neptune, the most distant planet (thanks to the recent demotion of Pluto from the planetary ranks) takes approximately 165 Earth years to revolve around the Sun.

Rubin, not unnaturally, expected stars to follow roughly the same behavior pattern: the farther away a star was from the center of the galaxy, the longer it would take to go around the galaxy's center. She was stunned to find that, in general, that was not the case. She found numerous examples in which the rotation speed remained essentially constant no matter how far the star was from the galactic center.

In order to explain this using the well-developed theories of gravitation, there had to be extra mass—and it was easy to compute the shape and distribution this mass needed to have in order that the stellar rotation curves should have the observed parameters. Unfortunately, nobody could find any evidence of the existence of this mass, other than the gravitational effect it has on stars. It emits no electromagnetic radiation whatsoever, and we have tried to detect it at a variety of wavelengths, from those longer than visible light to those much shorter. No luck. Not only is this matter invisible (in the sense that it emits no radiation in the visible portion of the spectrum), it is undetectable—at least so far. We're pretty sure it's there (it has an unquestioned gravitational effect) but we can't see it. It goes by the name *dark matter.*

Does dark matter exist? If it doesn't, there is something radically wrong with Einstein's Theory of General Relativity, which so far has withstood every challenge. So the challenge is to find and explain dark matter. There are several different competing explanations, but as yet, there is no clear winner. What is equally surprising is that there seems to be a lot more dark matter than ordinary matter in the Universe—for every kilogram of ordinary matter, there are four or five kilograms of dark matter.

But it's not just matter that is dark. The most recent Nobel Prize in Physics, given in 2011, was for the discovery in 1998 that the expansion of the Universe was accelerating, rather than slowing down. This result was completely unexpected, and, as of this moment, completely unexplained. The culprit, if that is the appropriate word, is now referred to as *dark energy*; dark energy is even more unknown than paranormal phenomena. Paranormal phenomena (telepathy, psychokinesis, remote viewing) have been categorized and scrutinized for more than a century. Dark energy has only been known to exist for a little more than a decade, yet it gets a Nobel Prize. Why not paranormal phenomena?

As far as I can tell, there has never been a Nobel Prize given in physics for *unconfirmed* phenomena. Einstein's Theory of General Relativity was propounded in 1915, and Einstein was awarded the Nobel Prize in Physics in 1921, but the award was given "for his services to Theoretical Physics, and especially for his discovery of the law of the photoelectric effect." Sir Arthur Eddington led an expedition in 1919 that produced results confirming the Theory of General Relativity, but the Nobel Committee was apparently sufficiently unimpressed that this took a back seat to the photoelectric effect, which Einstein had explained in 1905. Paul Dirac predicted the existence of antimatter in 1928, but it wasn't until it was actually discovered in 1932 that Dirac was awarded the Nobel Prize (in 1933).

One thing is certain: the moment that a psi force is actually discovered and verified, or any form of Crookes's new forces needed to explain the work of the Universe, it will make the discoverer an outstanding favorite to win a Nobel Prize. I must admit, I find it hard to believe in a psi force or any new force. However, one possible explanation for dark energy is a hypothetical fifth force known as quintessence. Like electricity, quintessence is presumed to have the property that it can be either attractive or repulsive. However, it has the bizarre property that it is either completely attractive or completely repulsive, and is presumed to have switched to completely repulsive 10 billion years ago. This may indeed be true, but I find ESP, telepathy, and even remote viewing to be equally credible.

Roughly 50 years ago, we discovered that the Universe had originated with a Big Bang, and we were fairly confident we knew its general overall structure. Now we believe the Universe is about 5 percent ordinary matter and energy, 25 percent dark matter, and 70 percent dark energy.[3] In other words, we have no idea what 95 percent of the Universe is. Although I feel it's unlikely this would affect the reality or unreality of paranormality phenomena, I don't think you can make a judgment like that with a high degree of confidence, especially considering that at the moment we have no explanation for 95 percent of the Universe.

But it should be clearly understood that the existence of dark matter and dark energy do not support the existence of paranormal phenomena any more than quantum mechanics does. I worry that quantum mechanics is old hat, and that someone who wrote "recent discoveries in quantum physics support the existence of paranormal phenomena" is going to revise this and write "the recent discovery of dark energy supports the existence of paranormal phenomena." We have no idea if it has any effect at all.

A Common Denominator

I think there are two possibilities for paranormal phenomena that might actually stand up: ESP and telepathy. Remote viewing belongs to the same general family of phenomena, but I feel it is less likely to be a valid phenomenon for reasons I will discuss later. These three have this in common: they all deal with the acquisition of information.

This is, so we are told, the Age of Information. We have progressed (if that is the word) to an economy that is focused more and more on the production and consumption of information. Google, Microsoft, Facebook, and Twitter among others are major corporate entities that are almost exclusively concerned with the production and dissemination of information.

It's not that information is so totally new. The production and dissemination of information has been a major concern of both individuals and societies. The Greeks and Romans did it on parchment scrolls, and the Chinese did it on paper. The printing press, invented in the middle of the 15th century by Johann Gutenberg, enabled the mass production of books, magazines, and newspapers. Until the end of the 19th century, the printed word and the hand-drawn picture were the chief means of storing and spreading information.

With the perfection of the camera and the introduction of radio, the amount of information that could be stored and disseminated accelerated during the first part of the 20th century. It moved into high gear in the mid-20th century with television, and into overdrive, where it is now, with the explosion of readily available computers and the development of the Internet in the late twentieth century. When one reads stories from the late 1930s and 1940s about what the world of the future would be like, it is amazing that they were predicting such things as robots and aircars, but nobody seems to have envisioned computers or the Internet. It would seem that with the almost infinite storage capabilities afforded by modern computers and the ability to transmit large quantities of information at near light speed, we are reaching the limit of what can be done with information. However, as the great physicist Leo Szilard once remarked, prediction is difficult—especially of the future.

The importance of information made it almost certain that at some stage, scientists would undertake analyzing information with the same tools that had brought them success in examining matter and forces. The landmark work in this area was a paper written in 1948 by Claude Shannon, entitled "A Mathematical Theory of Communication."[4] It was published in two parts in the Bell System Technical Journal, and focused on a very important problem: how best to encode the information a sender wishes to transmit. I was somewhat surprised to discover that Shannon had his puckish side, as in the 1960s I owned a copy of a toy that he had invented. It was a rectangular black box with a switch on one side. When you flipped the switch on, a lid on the box opened, and a mechanical finger came out and flipped the switch back to off. The finger then retreated into the box and the lid closed.

Shannon is also responsible for the idea that the fundamental unit of information is the bit, a digit which is 0 or 1. Just as elements are the basic chemical units of the Universe or cells are the basic biological units of living beings, bits are the basic units of information. Eight bits, strung together, are known as a byte. There are 256 possible bytes, from 00000000 through 11111111, and together they are used to represent all the common characters of English, as well as other important symbols. A capital "A," for instance, is represented as 01000001. This is what your computer stores; nowadays a computer selling for less than $500 will have a hard drive capable of storing at least a terabyte of information: 1,000,000,000,000 bytes. That's a truly awesome amount of information. This book contains roughly 70,000 words (and some other symbols, including blank spaces), but if we assume each word has about 6 bytes that's 420,000 bytes. Doubling that and rounding up to 1,000,000 bytes seems more than capable of being sufficient storage for this book, so a modestly-priced computer is capable of storing well over 1,000,000 books the size of this one. That's utterly staggering, at least to someone who started work in the 1950s on computers which had about 20,000 bytes of storage, roughly the amount needed for a single chapter of this book.

There's a mind-boggling amount of information in the Universe, but one thing about information is that it needs to be interpreted. Our eyes, in conjunction with our brain, decode the visual information that we receive; the same thing happens with our other senses as well. We know that visible light constitutes only an extremely small segment of the entire electromagnetic spectrum; the Universe is sending out information from low-frequency radio waves to ultra-high-frequency gamma rays. For the most part, we are not equipped, in terms of sense organs or brain function, to decode this information. It can certainly affect us; gamma radiation is lethal in large enough quantities, but for the most part we are blind to it.

Having the right interpretation equipment is extremely important. All the material that is stored on our computers—the documents and photographs, the spreadsheets, music, and videos—is in bytes, which as we have seen are just strings of 0s and 1s, but the information must be decoded. We know, for example, that if a file is labeled "rainbow.jpg," the ".jpg" tells us—and more importantly, the computer—that it is a JPEG image (most likely of a rainbow). If you've ever decided to rename such a file rainbow.doc and tried to read it, it's gibberish.

Information can be encoded at many different levels. One way that this can be done is illustrated by the idea of equidistant letter sequences (ELS) which recently came into prominence as the basis for Bible codes. The idea is simple, and is based on 2 numbers. An ELS code such as (3,4) says to start with the 3rd letter of the text, and then look at every 4th letter thereafter. If the (3,4) code is applied to the word "information," the word "fan" can be seen hidden within it. In order to see this clearly, the key letters that are part of the (3,4) code are capitalized: inFormAtioN.

The popular book *The Bible Code*[5] hypothesized that messages purporting to tell the future can be found by scrutinizing the Bible using certain ELS codes. The book claimed that it was statistically very unlikely for certain messages to be seen using this method by sheer chance. Other authors, somewhat skeptical of this idea, took popular books such as *Moby Dick* or *War and Peace* and used ELS codes to find similar messages. Numerologists sometimes claim that similar messages can be found by looking at the digits of important numbers such as pi; this idea was used not only in the film *Pi* but also in Carl Sagan's book *Contact*,[6] about man's first meeting with extraterrestrials. However, mathematicians have demonstrated that if you look far enough in certain numbers (known as *normal numbers*), every possible sequence of numbers can be found. Properly interpreted, the digits can be found to tell your life story—even the part that happens after you finish this book—and that story will be repeated infinitely often in the number! If you are a numerologist, what could be more wonderful than knowing that the complete history of the Universe—both present and future—is told in the digits of every single normal number. Of course, we'll never be able to interpret it.

The idea of encoding information plays an important part in transmitting information. The two most popular ways of sending and receiving radio messages are known as amplitude modulation (AM) and frequency modulation (FM). The sound wave that is generated by the radio broadcast—music, speech, or whatever—is not the actual wave that is communicated from the radio station to your receiver. In AM, the actual sound is encoded by varying the strength of the signal (its amplitude) and then adding a carrier wave to produce a wave that can be communicated over long distances. Obviously, you cannot speak loudly enough to be heard at distances of more than a few hundred feet or so, but a radio broadcast can be heard (with appropriate instruments) hundreds or even thousands of miles away. Once the AM signal reaches your radio, the receiver subtracts the carrier wave and then decodes the original sound wave by reading the variation in strength of the resulting signal.

How do we know that the messages that we receive do not have information encoded within it? I do not know to what extent this topic has been explored from a scientific standpoint. There are certain types of messages that are sent in Nature that are relatively straightforward. Examples of such messages abound. Every chemical element has a characteristic absorption spectrum; when light is shined through it, the element absorbs light of certain frequencies. When we see a rainbow, we do not see any lines in it. But when light is shined through a gas of a certain element, black lines appear where the element absorbs the light of that frequency. This information is the same no matter where the element is located (although the speed at which the element is moving towards or away from us can shift the location of the lines). DNA, however, is a vastly more complicated substance, and biologists are continually unearthing new surprises in the different levels of information contained within the DNA molecule. So Nature sometimes sends simple messages, and sometimes messages within messages.

The next question is, Can we as human beings decode those messages within messages? Well, we already do, and so do many other creatures on this planet. Consider something simple such as color. As we have mentioned, visible light only comprises an extremely small part of the electromagnetic spectrum. The color "red" is a label we have attached to a particular small segment of the electromagnetic spectrum; there are different shades of red, but most of us can see a color and identify it as red no matter whether it is maroon, burgundy, rose, or any of the other variations on the theme of "red."

When you think about it, that's fairly amazing. What is also amazing is that evolution has endowed us with sensory and processing information that translate that range of the electromagnetic spectrum into "red." First, our eyes are the sensory receptors for red—we don't hear red or smell red, we see red. Second, a large portion of our brain is devoted to taking the information acquired by our eyes and processing it into "red." We know that some of this processing takes place in our brain, because other animals who have very similar eyes—but very dissimilar brains—do not perceive color differences. So it could be argued that "redness" is a message that overlies the "vibration message" that characterizes that particular portion of the electromagnetic spectrum.

But we humans have also imbued "red" with meaning. "Red" means "stop" or "danger" in some cultures. Of course, that's a convention that the human race has adopted, but it's also a convention that the animal kingdom has adopted as well. In some species, "red" says "I'm dangerous" or "I'm poisonous." There are even secondary levels of information corresponding to the ways that colors are placed. There are two types of snakes which have bright red transverse bands—the deadly coral snake and the harmless milk snake. The coral snakes have red bands next to yellow bands, but the milk snakes have red bands next to black bands. In case you ever encounter one or the other, and are wondering how to remember, there's a useful mnemonic: "Red next to yellow can kill a fellow, but red next to black is a friend of Jack."

A great deal of information is sent by waves. What we call "sound" consists of waves of alternating rarefactions and compressions of the atmosphere; our ears interpret them as sound. What we call "light" consists of electromagnetic waves in a specific portion of the electromagnetic spectrum; our eyes interpret them as colors, and our brains sort these colors into recognizable patterns (and some unrecognizable ones, such as paintings by abstract artists or unrecognizable graffiti). However, it is possible to send information by other electromagnetic vibrations; we do it all the time with radio waves and microwave transmissions. The Universe is sending out information to us in the form of vibrations in other portions of the electromagnetic spectrum. We even have dedicated instruments to learn about the Universe by receiving this information. From microwaves, we learned about the Big Bang, and from gamma rays, we learned about quasars.

There is a significant difference between sound waves and electromagnetic waves. Sound waves are compressions and rarefactions in the direction in which the wave is moving, whereas electromagnetic waves vibrate in a plane perpendicular to the direction of motion. One way to visualize the difference is to imagine two people walking in a straight line and carrying a stretched bungee cord between them. A sound wave can be visualized by assuming that the distance between the two people alternately decreases and increases; this changes the amount of stretching of the bungee cord. The stretching corresponds to the compressions and rarefactions of the atmosphere, and occurs in the direction in which the people are walking. With an electromagnetic wave, you need to imagine that someone plucked it as if a guitar string had been plucked; the bungee cord will vibrate up and down in a plane that is perpendicular to the direction in which the people are walking. Moreover, there are infinitely many different angles at which the bungee cord could have been plucked—perpendicular to the ground, parallel to the ground, at a 45-degree angle to the ground, etc. This angle is referred to as the polarization of the wave.

Our ears can detect differing sounds, and our eyes can detect differing colors, but we are also sensitive to the effects that occur as the result of the differing polarization of light waves. Polarizing sunglasses enable us to see contrast more clearly and reduce glare, and some 3D movies are produced using polarization to achieve the 3D effect.

The importance of this is that polarization adds an additional dimension to electromagnetic vibration, and this additional dimension can be used to transmit or receive information. Many animals are able to recognize polarization of sunlight; bees use it to orient their dances in which they communicate the location of flowers that other bees in the hive can visit. Pigeons were originally thought to use polarization to navigate; later it was felt that this ability resulted from sensitivity to the Earth's magnetic field, but recently even this idea has been cast into doubt. At the moment, we are not certain how homing pigeons find their way home.

ESP

Of the three candidates I still have on the table as possible paranormal phenomena, the one that I feel is the most likely to actually be recognized as legitimate is ESP. There are several reasons for this, the first being that ESP is not really well-defined. Is the ability to see beyond the normal color range (from blue to red) or to hear lower or higher-pitched sounds than the normal range of audibility an example of ESP? Most people would say not. But suppose that we were able to sense earthquakes in advance because we were able to detect vibrations that signal an earthquake's future occurrence. This ability might initially be classified as ESP, but once thoroughly analyzed, it would no longer be regarded as extrasensory, because sensitivity to vibration occurs in sight, hearing, and touch (smell and taste are sensitivity to certain chemicals).

Although Taylor cites studies which show that humans cannot detect even strong magnetic fields,[7] there are recent studies that show we may indeed be sensitive to them. This would lie outside what we currently consider to be the five senses, but it would just be an additional sense. When I was growing up, we were told there were four basic types of taste buds: salty, sour, bitter, and sweet. Recently a fifth has been discovered, known as umami (which is also known as savory; it's what makes foods with MSG tastier). Was this ESP before it was discovered? No, it's just an extension to the realm of sensory perception.

Another possible explanation for ESP is that ESP is a suite combining sensory input from one or several of the five senses and the integration of them in the brain. I'm not sure whether intuition is considered to be a paranormal capability, but it is certainly a phenomenon that almost every one of us has experienced. One definition of intuition is that it is the ability to know something instinctively, without the necessity for conscious reasoning. This might seem that it puts it in the realm of ESP. However, there are a lot of things that we know without the necessity for conscious reasoning that probably don't come under the heading of intuition. Many of the dangers that confront us, such as a falling object, prompt quick reactions without conscious reasoning. Experienced drivers react to potential problems without consciously thinking about them. Whether we "know" to get out of the way of a falling object, or whether we just do it without "knowing," makes a big difference in whether intuition is involved.

Blink,[8] by Malcolm Gladwell, is an extremely popular book about how some decisions are made in the first two seconds—snap judgments that are made without rational analysis. Some high-ranking business leaders listen to all the facts that go into making a decision, but then rely on "gut feeling" to come up with the correct call. Confronted with a large bet at poker, many top professionals rely on "table feel" to decide whether they should call, raise, or fold.

We may call it intuition, but we are processing information; we are just not consciously aware that we are actually processing that information. However, the argument can be made that every one of the decisions above is simply an integrated evaluation of sensory information. The businessman has a database of past decisions—either his own or others—which have aspects in common with the decision he faces. The poker player makes his judgment on past experience of similar situations and/or his knowledge of the individual who has made the bet. Possibly none of these individuals can spell out in detail the reasons for their decisions, but it is reasonably likely that a dispassionate individual who had time to lay out all the details surrounding those decisions would come to similar conclusions for similar reasons. Intuition is not so much the gathering of information as it is the processing of that information, and it is quite literally extra-sensory.

Telepathy

Where does intuition leave off and the paranormal begin? Intuition is the processing of information we have, but telepathy represents the acquisition of information to which we do not obviously have access. However, my guess is that at some time in the future we will have access to that information, especially if we consider the possibility of mechanically-aided telepathy. This was actually a key plot point in the movie *Firefox*, about an advanced Soviet fighter plane which was controlled telepathically by the pilot.

We are already capable of brain studies pinpointing regions of increased activity when the subject's thoughts are linked with certain topics; that's partly where the expressions "left-brained" and "right-brained" come from. Obviously, there are physical differences in your brain when you are thinking about your job, about your personal life, or about sports events—different connections are being made in your brain. Do these different connections produce detectable differences outside the brain? I would think so, and I would think that at some stage we would produce technology which could detect these differences. After all, we currently have projects to produce visual images of planets circling stars light years away from us, as well as analyzing the chemical composition of their atmospheres. I don't think that the problem of detecting differences generated by thought patterns is beyond our eventual reach. The problem of mapping these differences to specific thoughts is also one of significant difficulty, but given enough time I think it is well within the reach of future technology. I'm not sure we'll ever reach the point that we'll be able to tell whether you are thinking about corn flakes rather than raisin bran, but I am certain that we'll reach the point that we can tell you are thinking about food rather than football, and we may reach the point that we can tell you are thinking about breakfast rather than lunch.

Will we ever be able to do this without technological assistance? Now we're reaching into the realm of the legitimately paranormal. I'm skeptical; I really think that in order to carry this off we would need to demonstrate the existence of something like a psi force. I think there is a longshot possibility that a psi force, or something like it, might manifest itself through the unknowable relationships between measurable physical parameters, but that's just a guess.

As a personal note, I'm not looking forward to telepathy. There is always a downside to technological innovation, and one of the downsides to easier interpersonal communication such as we enjoy today is the deterioration of privacy. Unless you pay by cash, all your purchases are tracked. Your GPS device knows where your car is, and every e-mail or text message that you ever send is a part of the permanent record. Absolutely the last frontier of privacy is your own private thoughts, and my guess is that they may not stay private forever.

Remote Viewing

I mentioned early in the book that a doctor friend of mine has walked into rooms knowing what he would see, even though he has never been there. Although I think that the most likely explanation of this is the same one that explains Bridey Murphy—he's seen a picture of the room or heard a description, and is not consciously aware of it—there is the possibility that somehow he has accessed information about the room through some other means. This information is clearly a part of the Universe, but how has he managed to access it without having it conveyed to him through the usual channels by which we obtain information?

I don't know, and although I could hazard a guess based on various ideas I've seen in science fiction, I think the most likely explanation for remote-viewing experiences is the statistical explanation discussed in the previous chapter for precognition. For every one such experience, there are many for which people who think they have seen something get it completely wrong, but don't bother to report it. After all, man bites dog is news, dog bites man is not. The Puthoff-Targ results on remote viewing have been largely discredited, and I don't know any other attempts that have done well. After all, the government is happy to dump huge sums of money into totally useless projects; when it pulls the plug on something such as the military remote-viewing projects, that's a real indication that there's nothing there to justify a further expense.

Every different arrangement of stuff creates different information, but without adequate technology, we cannot always obtain that information. We need X-ray machines and magnetic resonance imagers in order to find out what's going on inside your body. The major difference between remote viewing and telepathy is that we already have the technology to accomplish remote viewing, although taking satellite photographs doesn't actually constitute remote viewing in the paranormal sense. Because we know what technology is required, the gap between required technology and human attributes—and it is huge—can be assessed with considerable accuracy. We don't yet have the technology for telepathy, and so we are not as capable of making that judgment.

Summary

At the end of the last chapter, we left ESP, telepathy, and remote viewing on life support. I think that the millennium has not changed the situation with regard to remote viewing, but I think both ESP and telepathy will, at some stage, pass out of the realm of the paranormal and into the realm of accepted phenomena. However, they will do so for different reasons. I think that what will happen with regard to ESP is that we will discover that either there are other senses (such as the ability to sense magnetic fields) which we did not realize we have, or that the brain is capable of integrating sensory phenomena in ways that we currently do not realize. I also feel that the advance of technology will make telepathic communication, at some level, possible. In fact, I think that it is inevitable.

Removing the Mystery from the Paranormal

I have no great understanding of psychology, and there's a lot of human behavior that is a complete mystery to me. There seems to be a deep-seated desire in many people to experience some sense of wonder from phenomena they wish merely to accept, but not explain. They want telepathy to exist, but they don't want science to be able to explain it—as if the explanation of the phenomenon somehow ruins it. That makes absolutely no sense at all to a scientist, for whom the explanation of the phenomenon merely enhances the enjoyment of the phenomenon. Look at a snowflake under a microscopic; its hexagonal symmetry is exquisitely beautiful. It occurs because during the process of crystallization, attractive forces are maximized and repulsive ones minimized—this is an example of a scientific principle. Nature looks to do things with the least possible effort; in a sense, snowflakes are symmetric for a reason similar to the reason that water flows downhill rather than uphill.

Did learning that somehow destroy the beauty of the snowflake? I would think that it actually enhanced it. Even if it somehow detracted from the aesthetic beauty of a snowflake to know that it is a result of Nature performing processes economically during crystallization—although I don't see how that detraction could occur—I would think that it was compensated for by realizing that the beauty of a snowflake is just one example of a universal interconnectedness between processes, an interconnection that is exhibited by Nature performing processes economically.

Wishing that telepathy be a recognized phenomenon and still be classified as paranormal is akin to the famous couplet by Sir John Harrington:

Treason doth never prosper, what's the reason?

Why, if it prosper, none dare call it treason.[9]

As soon as a phenomenon becomes widely recognized as legitimate, it can no longer be paranormal. It can be unusual or even weird—there are lots of phenomena, such as two-headed animals, which fall under this classification—but they are not paranormal. You can't have it both ways.

The Paranormal Equation: The Final Word

I hope that this book has made a contribution to my original interpretation of its title—balancing the paranormal equation as it is interpreted by two groups with conflicting views: the scientists who have seen no ironclad evidence of anything that could genuinely be classified as paranormal, and those who believe that paranormal phenomena exist, even if science is presently unable to substantiate it.

However, there is another possible interpretation of the phrase "Paranormal Equation" that I described in the first few paragraphs of the Preface. There are many laws in science which are known by the equations that express these laws in mathematical terms. Maxwell's equations, for instance, express the laws governing the behavior of the electromagnetic field. Could there be a paranormal equation in this sense—an equation which somehow relates quantities that are currently considered to be within the realm of the paranormal?

Although I think this is an extreme long shot, there are two ways that it could happen. The first is to discover that Crookes was right, and there are still more forces needed to do the work of the Universe. There is absolutely no question that we are still in the infant stage as far as our knowledge of the work of the Universe is concerned. A century ago, the Universe was the Milky Way, which consisted of matter and energy, and we knew what forms both the matter and energy would take. The diameter of the Universe was about 100,000 light years—how long it takes light to cross from one side of the Milky Way to the other. Now, the diameter of the visible Universe is more than 100,000 times as large as we thought it was barely a century ago. Not only that, but with the recent discoveries on the expansion of the Universe, we have learned that most of the Universe consists of what we call "dark matter" and "dark energy"—and we have absolutely no idea what they are. Any member of the scientific community who predicted these developments a century ago (and none of them did) would have been regarded as—well, they would be regarded exactly the same way a scientist would be now if he or she said that new forces, such as a psi force, are still needed to do the work of the Universe.

The scientific community is more sophisticated now than it was a century ago. It has acquired an incredible amount of additional knowledge in that time, and it has also acquired more humility. It has learned that new doors are constantly being opened, and it is unwise to say what may—or may not—be hidden behind them. The vast majority of scientists undoubtedly subscribe to the belief that there is no such thing as the psi force. Many, including myself, would agree with Einstein, who said that although these ideas are interesting and worthy of investigation, all the forces of which science is currently aware attenuate with distance. Nonetheless, the history of science is that those discoveries which make the most impact are frequently the ones that contradicted the views of the experts.

We could never have made the discovery about dark energy without substantially improving technology beyond the level it was a century ago. Possibly, improvements in technology will enable us to find the elusive psi force, but I go along with the majority of scientists in harboring strong doubts that this will occur. If there is a paranormal equation, I think it is most likely to be hidden by an infinite Universe in the ranks of the unknowable, along the lines I have suggested in this book.

Nonetheless, there is still the chance that we might be able to glimpse a paranormal equation, even if it remains unknowable. There are currently a number of mathematical problems which may be undecidable propositions; I've discussed a couple of them in this book. Just because they are unknowable does not mean that we cannot get a hint of what they are. Consider, for instance, the

Collatz Conjecture: if you start with a number and divide by 2 if it is even or multiply by 3 and add 1 if it is odd, eventually you arrive at the number 1, no matter what number you start with. It wouldn't be called the Collatz Conjecture if there weren't some evidence that it is true.

If there is a paranormal equation in the sense I have described, it could be an equation regarding information transfer, possibly constructed by using as parameters mass, length, time, and electric charge. These are the parameters used in describing gravitation and electromagnetism, the two forces known to act at arbitrarily large distances. As with the Collatz Conjecture, we may well get a sense of what this paranormal equation would say. After all, the Collatz Conjecture arises as the result of an experiment, although it is an experiment in arithmetic rather than an experiment in measuring relations between physical parameters. The time may come when we have made enough measurements to conjecture a relationship involving information transfer that has all the earmarks of paranormality. I have no idea what this equation would look like. To be frank, I have no idea what ANY undecidable proposition using mass, length, time, and charge would look like, but, as I have said, I believe they exist, and I believe they exist as a consequence of there being an infinite Universe.

We are genuinely fortunate to live in a Universe in which the important laws—the ones that have so significantly enabled us to better our technology and improve our lives—are readily accessible to us. True, we have taken about 350 years (since Newton) to acquire this knowledge, and science holds the promise of even more fascinating and life-changing discoveries to be made. The discoveries science has made—and will make—are the real life-changing discoveries. But yet, in an infinite Universe, there is not just the possibility but the actuality that the truth is indeed out there but will forever remain a mystery, not because we will never know, but because we can never know.

Notes

Introduction

1. *www.brainyquote.com/quotes/quotes/v/voltaire145555.html.* The Website BrainyQuote is owned by BookRags Media Network.
2. Pierre-Simon de Laplace, *Theorie Analytique des Probabilites: Introduction,* v. VII, *Oeuvres (1812–1820).*
3. Frazier, *Paranormal Borderlands of Science*, 223.
4. Stein, James, *Cosmic Numbers* (New York: Basic Books, 2011).
5. Carl Sagan, *The Demon-Haunted World: Science as a Candle in the Dark* (New York: Ballantine Books, 1996).
6. *www.brainyquote.com/quotes/quotes/r/richardpf160383.html.* The Website BrainyQuote is owned by BookRags Media Network.
7. Frazier, *Paranormal Borderlands of Science*, 5–23.

8. Frazier, *Paranormal Borderlands of Science*, 63–64.
9. *www.quotationspage.com/quote/27537.html.* The Website Quotations Page is owned by Michael Moncur.

Chapter 1

1. *www.metrolyrics.com/somethings-happening-here-lyrics-buffalo-springfield.html.* The Website MetroLyrics.com was acquired in September 2011 by CBSiMG.
2. *www.brainyquote.com/quotes/authors/a/albert_einstein_2.html.* The Website BrainyQuote is owned by BookRags Media Network.
3. Stein, James, *How Math Explains the World* (New York: HarperCollins, 2008).
4. *www.brainyquote.com/quotes/quotes/d/donaldrums148142.html.* The Website BrainyQuote is owned by BookRags Media Network.

Chapter 2

1. Arthur C. Clarke, *Childhold's End* (New York: Ballantine Books, 2001).
2. Victor Mollo, *Bridge in the Menagerie* (New York: Hawthorn Books, 1967), 101.
3. *www.quotationspage.com/quote/23639.html.* The Website Quotations Page is owned by Michael Moncur.
4. *www.metrolyrics.com/superstition-lyrics-stevie-wonder.html.* The Website MetroLyrics.com was acquired in September 2011 by CBSiMG.
5. *http://articles.chicagotribune.com/2012-05-02/news/ct-talk-end-of-the-world-poll-0502-20120502_1_mayan-calendar-new-poll-mayan-prophecy.* The Website ChicagoTribune.com is owned by the Tribune Company.

6. *www.metrolyrics.com/aquarius-lyrics-hair.html.* The Website MetroLyrics.com was acquired in September 2011 by CBSiMG.

Chapter 3

1. *www.merriam-webster.com/dictionary/supernatural.* The Website Merriam-Webster.com is owned by Merriam-Webster, Inc.
2. James Houran, *From Shaman to Scientist* (Lanham, Md.: Scarecrow Press, 2004).
3. *http://dictionary.reference.com/browse/science.* The Website Dictionary.reference.com is owned by William Collins Sons & Co. Ltd.
4. *www.merriam-webster.com/dictionary/spirit?show=0&t=1337709767.* The Website Merriam-Webster.com is owned by Merriam-Webster, Inc.

Chapter 4

1. Robert Silverberg, *The Science Fiction Hall of Fame, Volume One, 1929-1964* (New York: Doubleday, 1970).
2. Paul de Kruif, *The Microbe Hunters* (Boston: Harcourt, 2002).
3. Ralph Waldo Emerson, *Nature: Addresses, and Lectures* (Boston: Houghton, Mifflin and Co, 1883).
4. *www.nasa.gov/mission_pages/kepler/news/kepler-16b.html.* The website NASA.gov is maintained by the National Aeronautics and Space Administration (NASA).
5. Michael Hart, *The 100* (New York: Citadel Press, 1992).
6. Lorenz, Edward. "Deterministic Nonperiodic Flow," *Journal of the Atmospheric Sciences* 20-2 (1963): 130-141.

7. G.J. Sussman, and J. Wisdom, "Numerical Evidence That the Motion of Pluto Is Chaotic," *Science* 241 (1988): 433–437.

Chapter 5

1. Lynn Steen, "The Science of Patterns," *Science* 240 (1988): 611–616.
2. Christopher Sykes, *No Ordinary Genius: The Illustrated Richard Feynman* (New York: Norton, 1995) 252.
3. Frazier, *Paranormal Borderlands of Science*, 241-262.
4. Frazier, *Paranormal Borderlands of Science*, 258.
5. *www.metrolyrics.com/aquarius-lyrics-hair.html.* The Website MetroLyrics.com was acquired in September 2011 by CBSiMG.
6. *www.nasa.gov/mission_pages/kepler/multimedia/images/kepler-22b-diagram.html.* The Website NASA.gov is maintained by the National Aeronautics and Space Administration (NASA).
7. *www.templetonprize.org/.* The Website Templetonprize.org is owned by the John Templeton Foundation.

Chapter 6

1. *www.todayinsci.com/K/Keynes_John/KeynesJohn-Quotations.htm.* The Website Todayinsci.com is maintained by Today in Science History.
2. Isaac Newton, *Philosophiae Naturalis Principia Mathematica.* (London: 1687).
3. Kerrie Hollihan, *Isaac Newton and Physics for Kids.* (Chicago: Chicago Review Press, 2009) 102.
4. *www.quotationspage.com/quote/862.html.* The Website Quotations Page is owned by Michael Moncur.

5. *www.quotationspage.com/quotes/Isaac_Newton.* The Website Quotations Page is owned by Michael Moncur.
6. Abell and Singer, *Science and the Paranormal*, 120.
7. Charles Darwin, *The Origin of Species* (New York: New American Library, 2003).
8. Abell and Singer, *Science and the Paranormal*, 122.
9. Bown, Burdett and Thurschwell, *The Victorian Supernatural*, 34.
10. Bown, Burdett and Thurschwell, *The Victorian Supernatural*, 24.
11. Upton Sinclair, *Mental Radio* (New York: A. & C. Boni, 1930).
12. Upton Sinclair, *The Jungle* (New York: Doubleday, Page, 1906).
13. Frazier, *Paranormal Borderlands of Science*, 62.
14. R. Targ and H.E. Puthoff, "Information transfer under conditions of sensory shielding," *Nature* 251 (1974) 602–607.
15. Taylor, *Science and the Supernatural.*
16. Taylor, *Science and the Supernatural*, 5.
17. Taylor, *Science and the Supernatural*, 5.
18. Frazier, *Paranormal Borderlands of Science.*
19. Frazier, *Paranormal Borderlands of Science*, 113–121.
20. John Taylor, *Super Minds*, (New York: Warner, 1977).
21. Russell Targ, *The Reality of ESP*, (Wheaton, Ill.: Quest Books, 2012).
22. *www.tcm.phy.cam.ac.uk/~bdj10/.* The Website tcm.phy.cam.ac.uk is maintained by the Cavendish Laboratory at Cambridge University.

23. Robin McKie, "Royal mail's guru in telepathy row," *The Guardian,* 30 September 2001, London.

Chapter 7

1. Arthur C. Clarke, *The Collected Stories of Arthur C. Clarke* (New York: Orb Edition, 2002), 301–308.
2. Hilbert's 23 problems, and their current status, can be found at Weisstein, Eric W. "Hilbert's Problems." From MathWorld–A Wolfram Web Resource. *http://mathworld.wolfram.com/HilbertsProblems.html.*

Chapter 8

1. Carl Sagan, *The Demon-Haunted World: Science as a Candle in the Dark* (New York: Ballantine Books, 1996) 201–218.
2. *www.pbs.org/wgbh/nova/physics/imagining-other-dimensions.html.* This Website was produced for PBS by station WGBH in Boston.
3. *www.skepdic.com/anthropic.html.* The copyright for this Website is owned by Robert Carroll. The page was designed by Christian Popa.

Chapter 9

1. *www.pbs.org/wgbh/nova/physics/spooky-action-distance.html.* This Website was produced for PBS by station WGBH in Boston.
2. Albert Einstein, Boris Podolsky and Nathan Rosen. "Can quantum-mechanical description of physical reality be considered complete?" *Physical Review* 47 (1935): 777–780.

3. John S. Bell, "On the Einstein-Podolsky-Rosen Paradox," *Physics 1* (1964): 195–200
4. Alain Aspect et al. "Experimental Tests of Realistic Local Theories via Bell's Theorem," *Physical Review Letters* (1981): 460.
5. *www.tu-harburg.de/rzt/rzt/it/QM/cat.html#sect5*. This Website is owned by the Technical University of Hamburg (Germany). The specific page is a translation of Schrodinger's original paper.
6. *http://in.answers.yahoo.com/question/index?qid=20090529131028AAd5VwP*. This Website is owned by Yahoo! Inc.
7. *http://mindpower-info.com*. This Website is owned by Mindpower-Info.com.
8. *http://deeptrancenow.com*. This Website is owned by Dr. Laura De Giorgio.

Chapter 10

1. Philip K. Dick, *The Man in the High Castle*, (New York: G.P. Putnam's Sons, 1962).
2. Bruce Rosenblum and Fred Kuttner, *Quantum Enigma: Physics Encounters Consciousness* (Oxford: Oxford University Press, 2006) 104.
3. *www.brainyquote.com/quotes/authors/n/niels_bohr.html*. The Website BrainyQuote is owned by BookRags Media Network.
4. *http://space.mit.edu/home/tegmark/multiverse.pdf*. This is a PDF file that can be downloaded. The Website space.mit.edu is maintained by the Massachusetts Institute of Technology.

Chapter 11

1. *http://en.wikipedia.org/wiki/Joseph_Banks_Rhine.* The Website Wikipedia.org is owned by Wikimedia Corp.
2. Taylor, *Science and the Supernatural*, 16.
3. Abell and Singer, *Science and the Paranormal*, 57.
4. *http://en.wikipedia.org/wiki/Edgar_Mitchell.* The Website Wikipedia.org is owned by Wikimedia Corp.
5. Taylor, *Science and the Supernatural*, 48.
6. *http://en.wikipedia.org/wiki/Stargate_Project.* The Website Wikipedia.org is owned by Wikimedia Corp.
7. *http://en.wikipedia.org/wiki/Remote_Viewing.* The Website Wikipedia.org is owned by Wikimedia Corp.
8. *www.geom.uiuc.edu/~banchoff/Flatland/.* This Website is a project of The Geometry Center at the University of Minnesota. The book *Flatland* is available through the page maintained by Prof. Thomas Banchoff of Brown University.
9. *www.brainyquote.com/quotes/authors/a/albert_einstein_7.html.* The Website BrainyQuote is owned by BookRags Media Network.
10. *www.poemhunter.com/poem/i-see-the-four-fold-man/.* C. Ekrem Teymur is the author of the Website Poemhunter.com.
11. Taylor, *Science and the Supernatural*, 17.
12. *www.pbs.org/wgbh/aso/databank/entries/dp67be.html.* This Website was produced for PBS by station WGBH in Boston.
13. *www.physics.ucla.edu/~cwp/articles/noether.asg/noether.html.* This Website is maintained by the Physics Department at the University of California in Los Angeles (UCLA).

Chapter 12

1. James Burke, *Connections* (New York: Simon & Schuster Paperbacks, 2007).
2. Daryl Bem and Charles Honorton, "Does Psi Exist? Replicable Evidence for an Anomalous Process of Information Transfer," *Psychological Bulletin* 115 (1994): 4–18.
3. *http://science.nasa.gov/astrophysics/focus-areas/what-is-dark-energy/.* The Website NASA.gov is maintained by the National Aeronautics and Space Administration (NASA).
4. Claude E. Shannon, "A Mathematical Theory of Communication" *Bell System Technical Journal* 27 (1948): 379–423, 623–656.
5. Michael Drosnin, *The Bible Code* (New York: Touchstone, 1998).
6. Carl Sagan, *Contact* (New York: Pocket Books, 1997).
7. Taylor, *Science and the Supernatural*, 69–72.
8. Malcolm Gladwell, *Blink* (New York: Little, Brown and Company, 2005).
9. *www.brainyquote.com/quotes/authors/j/john_harrington.html.* The Website BrainyQuote is owned by BookRags Media Network.

Bibliography

Abell, George O. and Barry Singer. *Science and the Paranormal.* New York: Charles Scribner's Sons, 1981.

Bown, Nicola, Carolyn Burdett and Pamela Thurschwell. *The Victorian Supernatural.* New York: Cambridge University Press, 2004.

Frazier, Kendrick. *Paranormal Borderlands of Science.* Amherst, N.Y.: Prometheus, 1981.

Houran, James. *From Shaman to Scientist.* Lanham, Md.: Scarecrow Press, 2004.

Taylor, John. *Science and the Supernatural.* New York: E.P. Dutton, 1980.

Index

A

B

C

N

O

P

Q

R

S

T

U

V

W

X

Z

About the Author

Dr. James Stein graduated from Yale in 1962 with a BA in mathematics, and received his PhD from the University of California at Berkeley in 1967. He is the author of more than 30 research articles on mathematics and the coauthor of textbooks on mathematics and strategic management, as well as several books on mathematics and science for the general public. His latest book, *Cosmic Numbers: The Numbers That Define Our Universe,* received many favorable reviews, including one from the *Wall Street Journal.* He has written op-ed pieces on mathematics education for the Los Angeles Times, and served on state and nationwide panels on mathematics education. He has also blogged for *Psychology Today* and the *Huffington Post,* and has won regional and national championships at contract bridge.

Dr. Stein lives in Redondo Beach, California.